Creating Protection Healing Grids with Quantum Energetics of Sun Portals and the Light Portals

BY EL KA

DISCLAIMER:
The information in this book is based on the author's
work with sacred geometry connected to creating
Fleur De Lis protection grids and making healing grids.
Every effort and attempt to ensure that this book includes
accurate information has been made on the part of the author,
however mistakes and / or inaccuracies may well exist. The author accepts
no liability or responsibility for any loss or damage caused or thought to be
caused by the advice or information provided in this book. It is
recommended that any advice given in this book be used in
conjunction with your own discernment and intuition.

www.seekingthetruthinr.wixsite.com/startravelermessages

BY EL KA

CREATING PROTECTION HEALING GRIDS WITH QUANTUM ENERGETICS OF SUN PORTALS AND THE LIGHT PORTALS

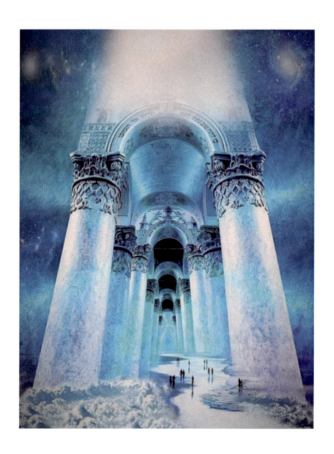

FOREWORD

This book seeks to explore EL KA's sacred geometry work exploring the creation of protection grids and healing grids connected with the Fleur De Lis, sun portals, light portals and also stargates in France.

DISCOVERING SACRED GEOMETRY WITH CREATION OF PROTECTION AND HEALING GRIDS

Introduction

I have recently taken a spiritual journey into discovering the beauty of working with sun portals light portals, solar eclipses as well as stargates with connection to sacred geometry that flows into the field of the Akashic Records and Light Language for healing. The inspiration of exploring looking at the inner structures of the sun portals, light portals, solar eclipses and stargates came when Kimberly Palm who is a spiritual teacher had shared with me several images of what looked like colored portals and rainbows in the sky in her photographs taken in Southern France in the regions of the village at Beynac-et-Cazenac in the area of the Dordogne River Perigord Noir by the Chateau de Beynac and at Rayol Canadel near Saint Tropez.

I was curious to see what was behind the bright colors of the sun energetics and beyond the rainbows even though there was no weather conditions to even create rainbows it seems that the portals were creating a harmonic frequency in the sky showing that portal activity is present in Southern France because of the sacred sites there and connection to the anchoring vibration of Mary Magdalene and Yeshua grounding energies.

When I started to look at the portal images from a sacred geometry perspective I saw the healing properties connected to the light field patterns in the portal grid sequencing. This inspired me to create the custom made sun portal, light portal, solar eclipse healing grids as well as the Fleur De Lis Protection Grids. These grids have energetic frequencies to raise energy levels, to heal the body, mind and the soul, create new opportunities for manifesting success and happiness in people's lives, to improve how someone is feeling, and to create an experience where we are protected in our lives by the sacred geometry grids that are illustrated in this book.

How to Connect and Work with the Protection and Healing Grids

All of the protection Fleur De Lis Grids are encoded with positive source field energies to provide intuitive guidance to protect people, homes, objects, and to shield against negative energies and beings so nothing can interfere with a person's soul, higher self, body and the mind. The protection from the grids can activate the shielding around the body and wherever you are in the home, land and other surroundings like the car or even traveling to other countries. Since the Fleur De Lis Grids have the energetic frequency for protection they also have the various colors, and symbols like stars and hearts with encoded light healing vibrations to provide healing for the mind, body and the soul. There are fifty Fleur De Lis Grids that can be selected to work with and you can set any intent for manifesting positive protection and healing. You can create your own protection and healing mantras to infuse into the grids with your focused intentions or just have the grids somewhere near you as they are already providing the protection and healing since they are energetically activated with these frequencies for such purposes.

To select which of the Fleur De Lis Grids vibrate the best with your energies hold your hands over the grids and tap into their frequencies with your thought consciousness to decide which grid you would like to work with for protection, healing or manifesting something to be created in your life. You can create customizable mantras for manifesting something positive to be achieved in your life or to change a situation that is not working for you, remove blockages, etc. with the Fleur De Lis Grids as they are charged with light codes for doing manifestation work.

The various Sun Portal, Light Portal, and Solar Eclipse Grids are encoded with healing frequencies as well they can be used to set any type of intent for protection, manifestation, meditation, etc. It is good to spend some time thinking about what intent and purpose you would like to create if you are thinking about making your own activation mantras to work with the grids then energetically infusing these intentions into the grids by writing out your mantras, speaking them out loud while holding both of your hands over the grid(s) in order to program the grid with these intents to set protection, healing, or to manifest something that is of a positive nature to help you in your life.

All of the grids have infinite energies of source field creation frequencies that anyone can tap into so they can work with the grids to customize their individual mantras for setting intent for protection, healing, manifestation, connecting with their inner wisdom, intuition, guidance, higher self, guides, etc. By studying each grid for its unique colors, symbols and the sacred geometry you will discover which grid from the sets calls to you for the work that you would like to do with the grid(s). Once you tap with your mind into the energies of the grids you will know which of these grids are the right ones for you to be able to connect with as you listen to your inner knowing, trust yourself with this guidance. It will lead you to understanding which grid is the one you should work with in order to set up your intentions and purposes. The grids are designed for anyone to work with based on intuition, thought consciousness, and feeling into the energies of the grids to be able to connect with their frequencies so that the grids can help you with positive learning of how to create intent for setting up your own manifestation techniques, being able to create mantras for healing, protection, etc.

There are several examples provided for healing and protection mantras that are guidance techniques that you can work with for creating your own unique words of power to facilitate protection, healing and manifestation.

You can expand any of these guidance techniques and add in your own words to connect with the grids or follow the guidance to do the healing and protection work. The grids are designed to allow everyone to connect with their creative processes and to expand their mind and soul to tap into the holographic universe of quantum consciousness so that you can explore infinite possibilities without having any limits when working energetically and physically with the grids for your guided work. They can also add an element of meditation and clearing your mind of anything that is blocking your creative process by seeing the image of the grid in your mind during meditation and allowing it to clear the blockages so there is nothing standing in your way for your creative abilities to expand in your work.

Working with energy grids like the Fleur De Lis Protection Grids, Sun Portal, Light Portal and Solar Eclipse Grids does not require for anyone to put any crystals on these grids in any specific gridding patterns since these grids are already encoded with source field energetics for creating protection, healing and manifestation. If you do not have any crystals with you then the grids will work on their own for the purposes of protecting, healing and manifesting what is needed to be in your lives. However if you would like to add crystals to the grids it will add that unique energetic extra layer to enhance your intentions for the gridding processes when you work with the energetic frequencies of the grids for your highest good and wellbeing.

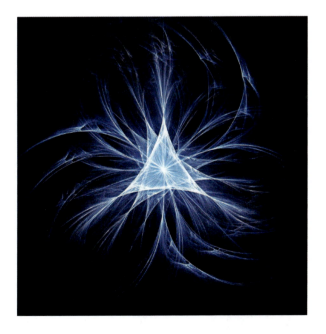

Fleur De Lis Protection Grids

The Fleur De Lis Protection Grids symbolize both soul and physical protection for the person and the home that they live in protecting them from negative energies, beings, and anything that is not of the highest good so nothing can harm the person while they have the protection grid(s) in their surroundings.

All the Fleur De Lis protection grids have the golden spiral energies of healing and protection as well as the blue spiral energies of good health and wellbeing for everyone that works with the protection grids. The vibrant colors of gold, yellow, blue, purple, white, orange, terracotta (brown & orange), red, etc. that are encoded in the protection grids combine frequencies for creating manifestation in achieving your life goals and successes as you are creator beings exploring your journeys in life, connecting with your higher self, spirit guides, intuitive wisdom, finding your life path meanings of soul purpose and mission by being in communication with your inner intuitive selves. Colors of the green blended with purple, pink, blue, white, orange, etc. represent the light body aspects and connecting with the rainbow body to center and ground for balance in meditation, connect with past lives and with the future self. The wings represent activation with soul wisdom as well as reaching the divine source communing with the angel guides. Aspects of the golden dragons, golden mantids and the frogs represent unity for soul balance and grounding as well as soul protection. The golden stars and hearts represent connecting with the universe on a soul level and understanding the universal knowledge that is being accessed as well as having the golden spiral of infinite healing vibrating its frequencies to heal on the whole level of embodiment through the soul, mind, and physical healing happening on the quantum vibrations encoded in the crystalline grids. This is what the protection and healing grids are energetically designed to help you to connect with.

Setting Intention to Create Protection with Fleur De Lis Grids

If someone is setting up protection with the Fleur De Lis symbols from the grid sets they would begin by connecting with the color frequency in the grid like in this grid for example you would connect with the golden spiral color frequencies to set a focused intention to protect yourself and shield yourself against any harm or negative beings by sending the golden spiral frequencies of both the Fleur De Lis and the stars to create an energetic shield around yourself so you are safely protected from anything not of the highest good.

As well the heart symbols can be utilized to create a loving and harmonious frequency of balance in your life so that you are free of stress or accumulating karma in your soul.

Setting Intention to Create Healing with Fleur De Lis Grids

If something physical is hurting like in the body, put your hands over the grid and focus your mind on the golden spiral healing energy of the Fleur De Lis symbols to direct the healing golden energy frequency towards what specifically hurts in the body to heal it with these color frequencies. Keep the vibrational healing focus on what has the imbalance in the body so that the energies of healing are flowing to those areas. With the healing of the Fleur De Lis energetics feel the pain dissipating and being completely healed and energized. The healing from the grid is creating a balanced energy for you which is for your highest good and wellbeing.

Fleur De Lis Protection Grid 1

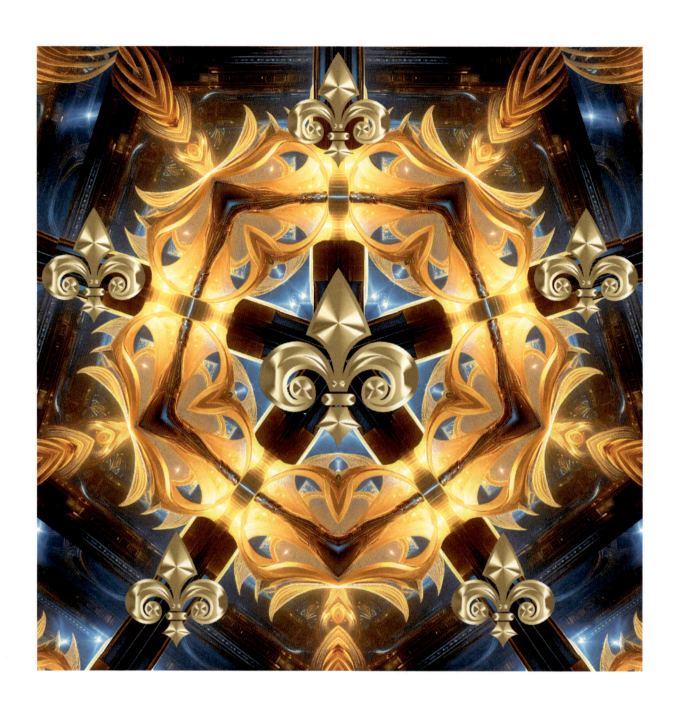

Fleur De Lis Protection Grid 2

Fleur De Lis Protection Grid 3

Fleur De Lis Protection Grid 4

Fleur De Lis Protection Grid 5

Fleur De Lis Protection Grid 6

Fleur De Lis Protection Grid 7

Fleur De Lis Protection Grid 8

Fleur De Lis Protection Grid 9

Fleur De Lis Protection Grid 10

Fleur De Lis Protection Grid 11

Fleur De Lis Protection Grid 12

Fleur De Lis Protection Grid 13

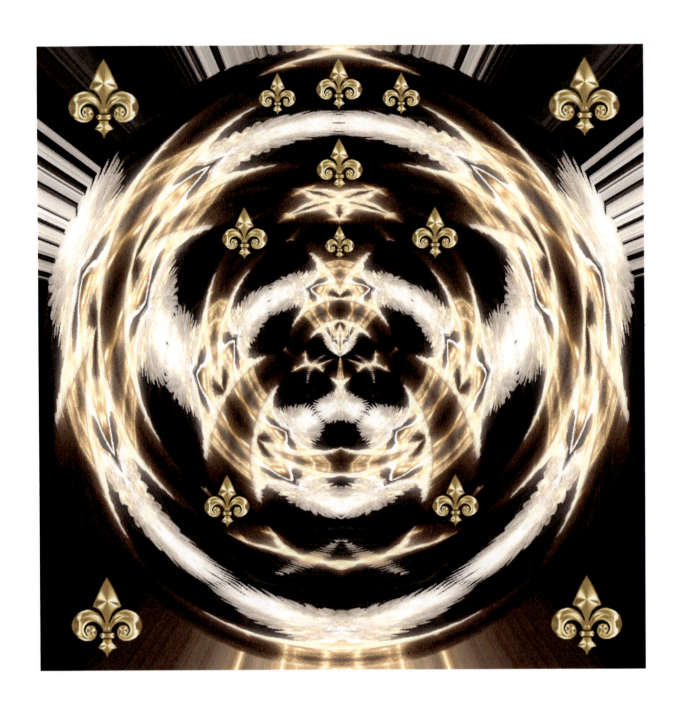

Fleur De Lis Protection Grid 14

Fleur De Lis Protection Grid 15

Fleur De Lis Protection Grid 16

Fleur De Lis Protection Grid 17

Fleur De Lis Protection Grid 18

Fleur De Lis Protection Grid 19

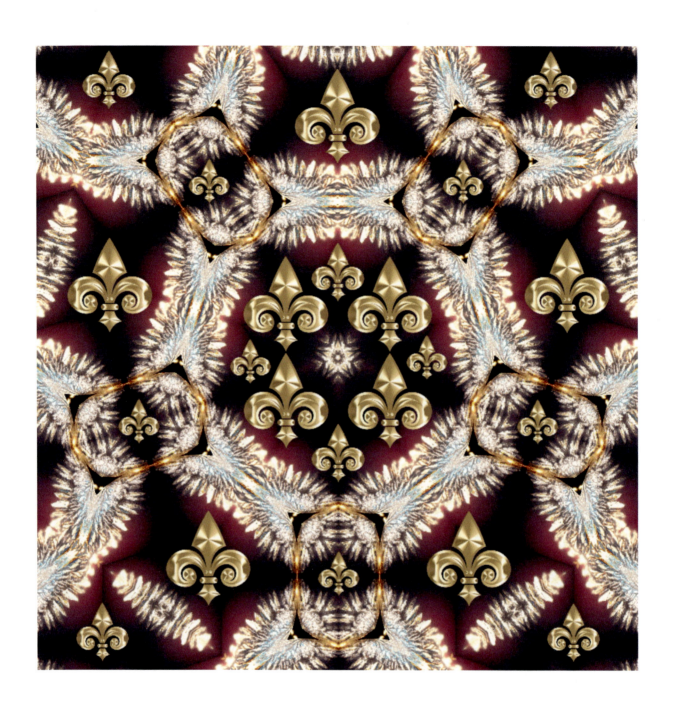

Fleur De Lis Protection Grid 20

Fleur De Lis Protection Grid 21

Fleur De Lis Protection Grid 22

Fleur De Lis Protection Grid 23

Fleur De Lis Protection Grid 24

Fleur De Lis Protection Grid 25

Fleur De Lis Protection Grid 26

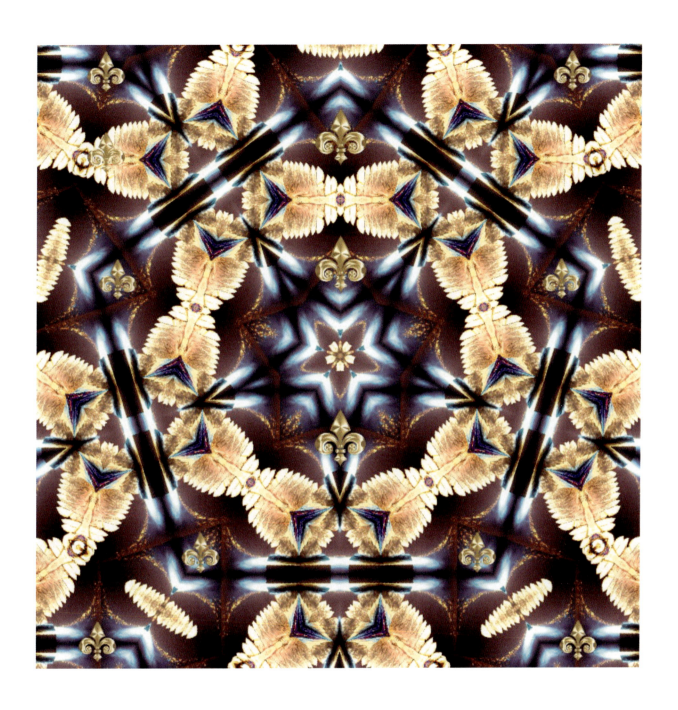

Fleur De Lis Protection Grid 27

Fleur De Lis Protection Grid 28

Fleur De Lis Protection Grid 29

Fleur De Lis Protection Grid 30

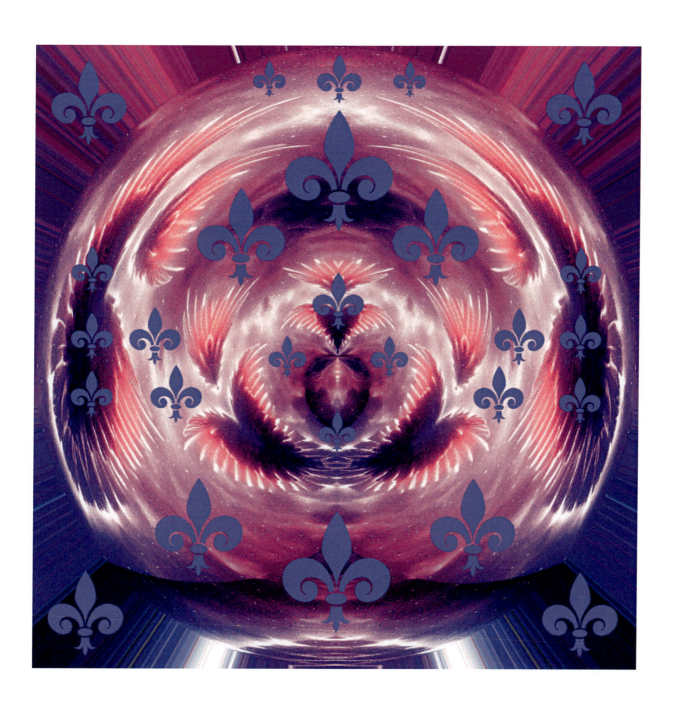

Fleur De Lis Protection Grid 31

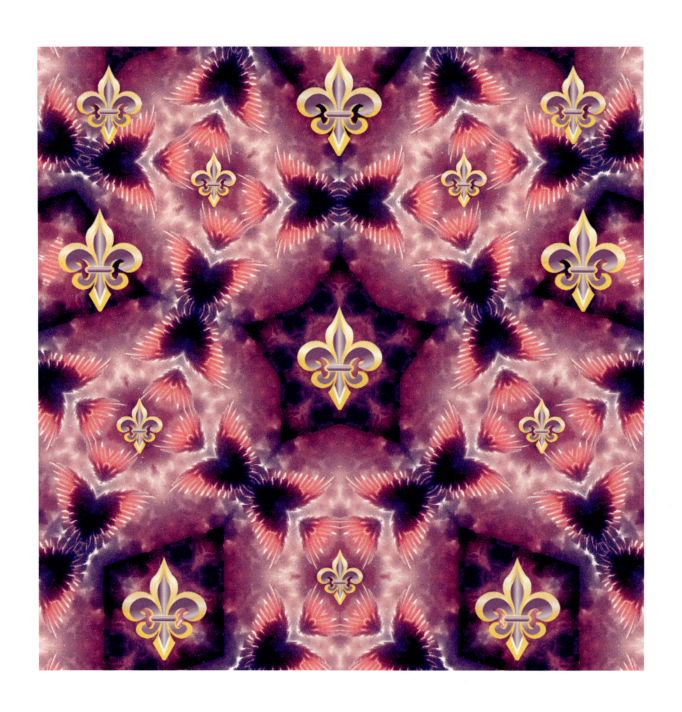

Fleur De Lis Protection Grid 32

Fleur De Lis Protection Grid 33

Fleur De Lis Protection Grid 34

Fleur De Lis Protection Grid 35

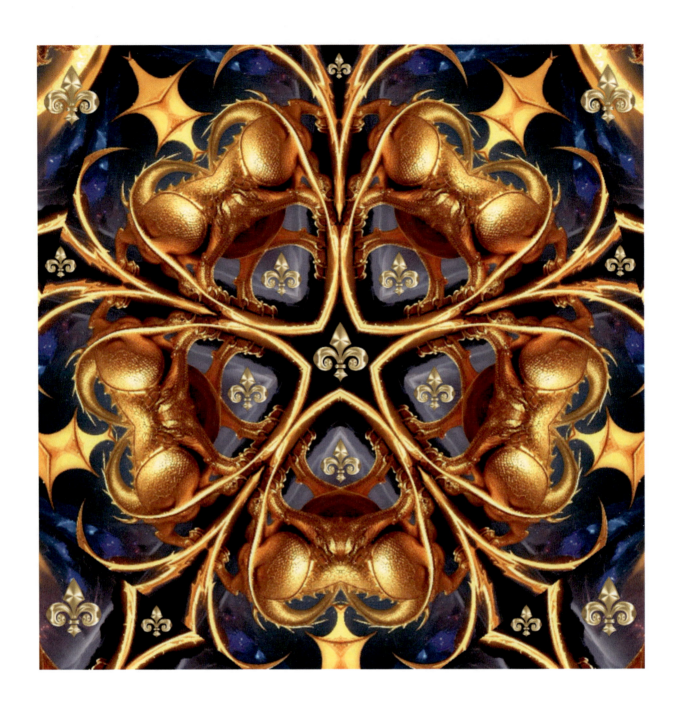

Fleur De Lis Protection Grid 36

Fleur De Lis Protection Grid 37

Fleur De Lis Protection Grid 38

Fleur De Lis Protection Grid 39

Fleur De Lis Protection Grid 40

Fleur De Lis Protection Grid 41

Fleur De Lis Protection Grid 42

Fleur De Lis Protection Grid 43

Fleur De Lis Protection Grid 44

Fleur De Lis Protection Grid 45

Fleur De Lis Protection Grid 46

Fleur De Lis Protection Grid 47

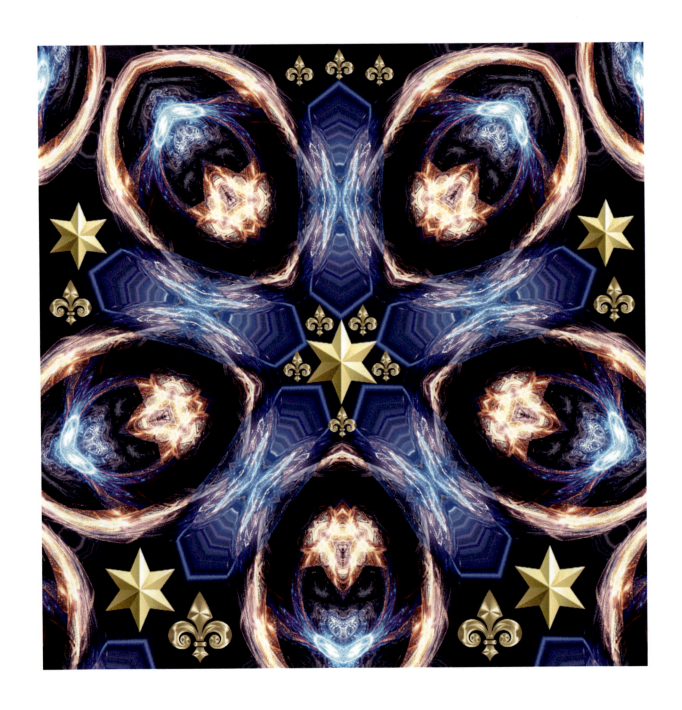

Fleur De Lis Protection Grid 48

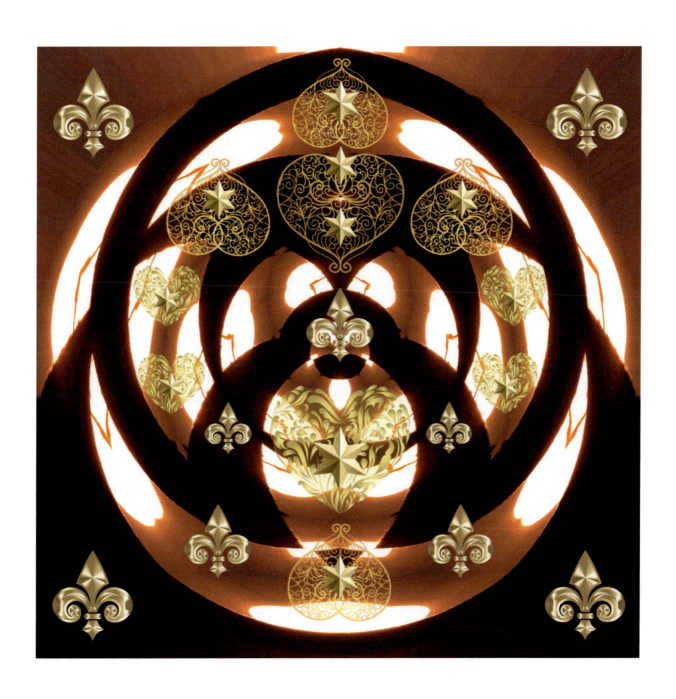

Fleur De Lis Protection Grid 49

Fleur De Lis Protection Grid 50

Dordogne River Perigord Noir Region in Southern France with Portals and Stargates

Recently Kimberly Palm was traveling in Southern France and she had visited the medieval village of Beynac-et-Cazenac in the area of the Dordogne River Perigord Noir by the Chateau de Beynac. She took pictures of the sun portals and stargates while traveling in these areas. When you focus in your screen on the oval shaped rainbow color object under the sun this is a portal for the high level light ships to come through for the (good ETs). There were a few of these sun portals in Southern France and (Kimberly Palm) photographed them many times while on her trip. These seem to be stargate portal images from France. The inspiration for the sun portal healing grids came from Kimberly's photographs of the sun portals.

The areas in the South of France have 70% forest lands and 1,001 chateaux castles. All the medieval villages date back to Roman times and also there are various caves where people lived for over 50,000+ years. There are three stories going underground into caves where people did art 50k years ago it was incredible the energies that were deep inside the Earth they were amazing. It felt like being inside the womb of mother Gaia.

Information By: **Kimberly Palm**

Village of Beynac with Sun Portals. Image by Kimberly Palm

Rayol Canadel near Saint Tropez in Southeastern France with Portals and Stargates

Recently Kimberly Palm was traveling in in the Rayol Canadel area near Saint Tropez in Southeastern France. She took pictures of what looks like rainbows in the sky however these are not rainbows as there was no moisture and it had been a very dry day and air had also been dry when these images were photographed by Kimberly Palm. The sun portal healing grids are inspired by Kimberly's sun portal photographs. Kimberly had felt the vibration of joyful expansion, filled with positive healing energy while visiting Rayol Canadel. There is also a specific beach which is the only one on the southern coast that has golden flecks in the sand and water as well as in the rocks that looks like 24k gold. In my discussion with Kimberly she mentioned that she is not sure if it is gold, fool's gold or mica but it was still the most beautiful golden sparkly beach that she had ever seen with an incredible portal up above it.

Information By: **Kimberly Palm**

Light Portals at Royol Canadel Southeastern France. Images by Kimberly Palm

Royol Canadel beaches in Southeastern France.

Sun Portal Healing Grids

The Sun Portal Healing Grids send regenerative frequencies that creating a high vibrational healing for the body, mind, and the soul to improve health, mood, happiness in life, and to manifest success. These sun portal grids have beautiful colors of blue, white, pink, purple to initiate balance and grounding for healing and meditation as well as to be in harmony with oneself as well as inspiring creativity and manifestation for creating your best life and timeline for achieving your goals.

Sun portals bring a spiritual wisdom from the upper densities and dimensions to help with human evolution of the mind and the body when the energetic frequencies from these portals emit a source field that connects us with divine healing, universal knowledge and we are able to download our positive light codes for expansion of the soul vibration to reach its highest potentials.

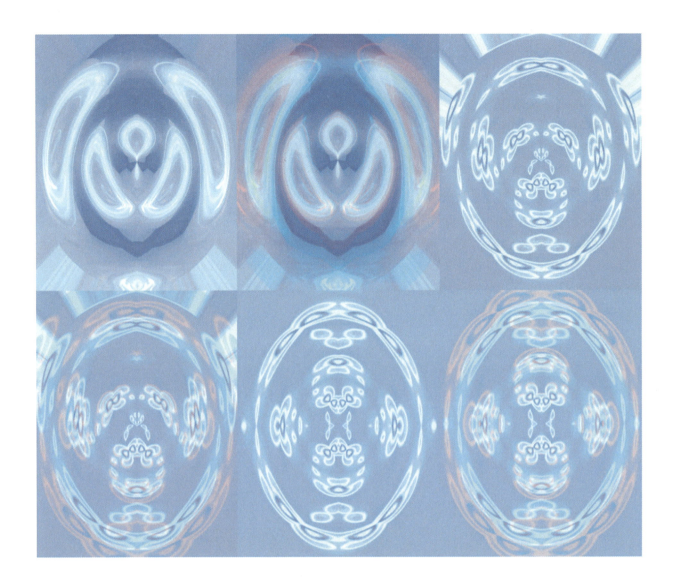

Working with All the Elements of the Sun Portal and Light Portal Grids for Creating Healing, Protection and Manifestation

When creating and doing energetic healing, protection, or manifestation work with the various elements of the sun portal and light portal grids connect to the colors, shapes, and the light coded frequencies within the sacred geometry symbols in the grids in order to set your focused intent and speak the words of power to embody your creation into reality. For example I set the intention to be completely healed this is for my highest good, I am receiving the healing energies to be free of any illnesses, diseases, and this healing facilitates being fully healthy in my divine state of existence. I am well and I am healed. If you are setting up house protection then set the intent of I focus on clearing any and all negative energies from my home, I clear all blockages within myself that have prevented me from being free and I work with the color frequencies in the grids I have chosen to create a shield around myself that keeps anything not of the highest good out of my home, living space, protecting my divine body and soul from any and all interferences keeping me always safe and guarded for my highest good and protection in this life.

Setting Up Having Positive and Focused Intention for Creating Healing, Protection and Manifestation in Your Work

It is important to always be as pure as possible in your divine state of being with your vibrational self before starting to do any type of energetic work where you will be connecting with setting up a purpose and an intent to do something on the spiritual levels. The first step is to clear your mind of all active thoughts so there are no distractions or interruptions when you are going to be setting up to do any type of focused intention for creating healing, protection or manifestation endeavors. Then you would spend some time deciding which grids you would like to work with and what is the purpose of your focused intention(s). What are you trying to create, manifest or accomplish in your life, what are your goals, desires and what would you like to achieve in the outcomes of working with the healing and protection grids. Which colors, symbols and other elements in the grids would you like to incorporate in your energetic work as well as becoming attuned to the frequencies of all the grids so that you will be familiar with the specifics of what each grid can help you to manifest for yourself on the energetic and physical scale as well as what it can do to improve something in your life. When there is honor and positive focus set in your intentions then there will be good results in the outcomes of your work.

Sun Portal Healing Grid 1

Sun Portal Healing Grid 2

Sun Portal Healing Grid 3

Sun Portal Healing Grid 4

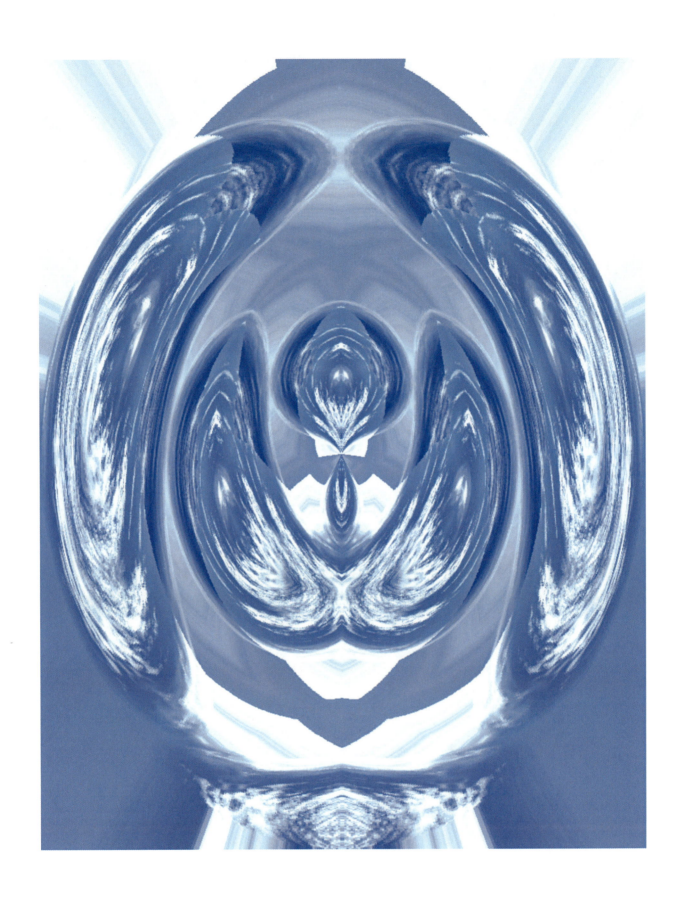

Sun Portal Healing Grid 5

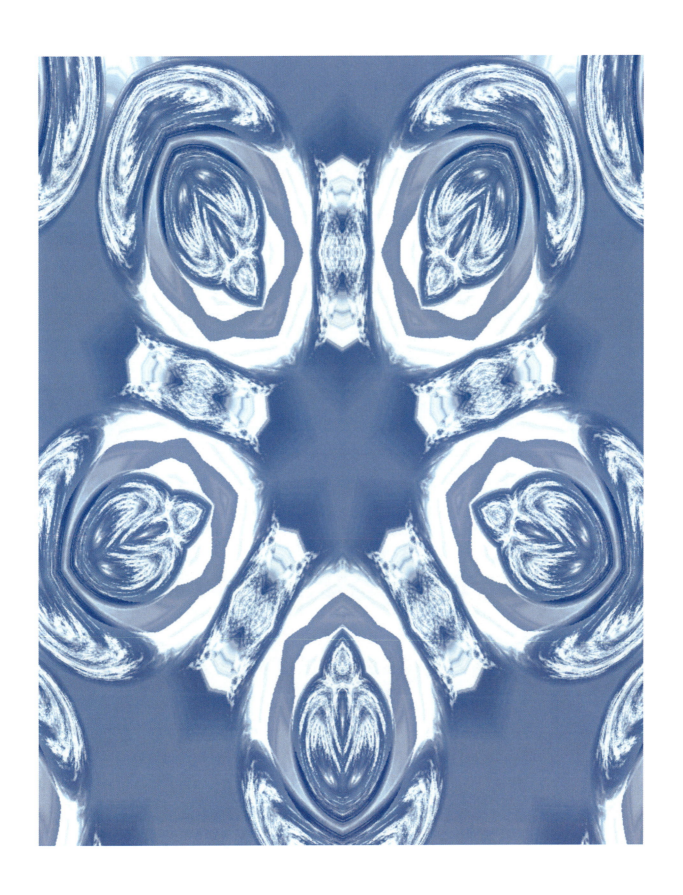

Sun Portal Healing Grid 6

Sun Portal Healing Grid 7

Sun Portal Healing Grid 8

Sun Portal Healing Grid 9

Sun Portal Healing Grid 10

Sun Portal Healing Grid 11

Sun Portal Healing Grid 12

Sun Portal Healing Grid 13

Sun Portal Healing Grid 14

Light Portal Healing Grids

The light portals can look like rainbows in the sky with various harmonics frequencies that activate the light spectrums within the coded light fields of the portals so that positive light beings like the Andromedans, Arcturians, Pleiadians, and Sirians can come to planets like Earth in their light ships in order to raise the light quotient on Earth and increase the source field energetic frequencies of the ley lines and raise the vibrational tuning fields within the pillars of light on the planet so that the planetary core light frequency is stable.

Light portal energetics can send healing frequencies to souls to heal the light codes within the body and mind as well as repairing the DNA codes within a living being.

Portals that consist of light frequencies are created by light fields this is part of the variation for elemental portal creation and part of the energy portal sequences that are calibrated for creation in portal travel and star frequency energetics when traveling in different densities or dimensions by way of quantum light sources that are the light portals.

Light Portal Healing Grid 1

Light Portal Healing Grid 2

Light Portal Healing Grid 3

Light Portal Healing Grid 4

Light Portal Healing Grid 5

Light Portal Healing Grid 6

Light Portal Healing Grid 7

Light Portal Healing Grid 8

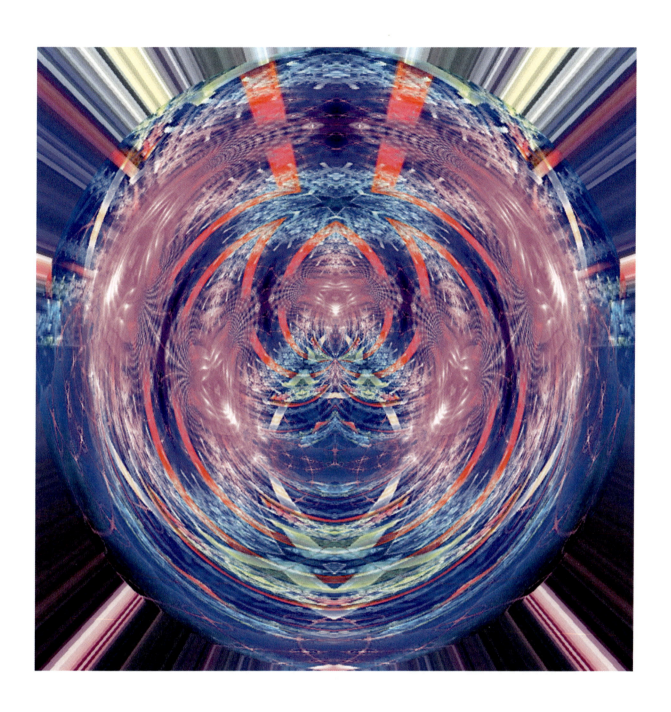

Light Portal Healing Grid 9

Light Portal Healing Grid 10

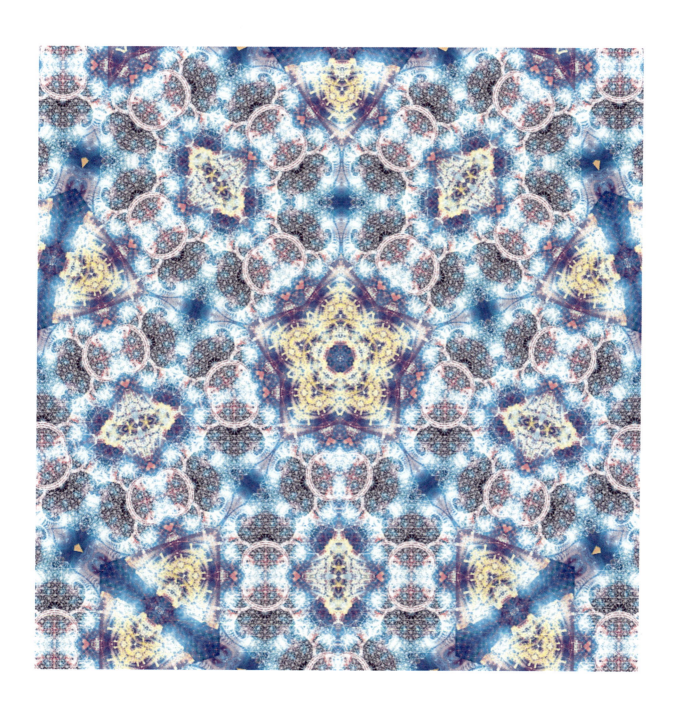

Light Portal Healing Grid 11

Light Portal Healing Grid 12

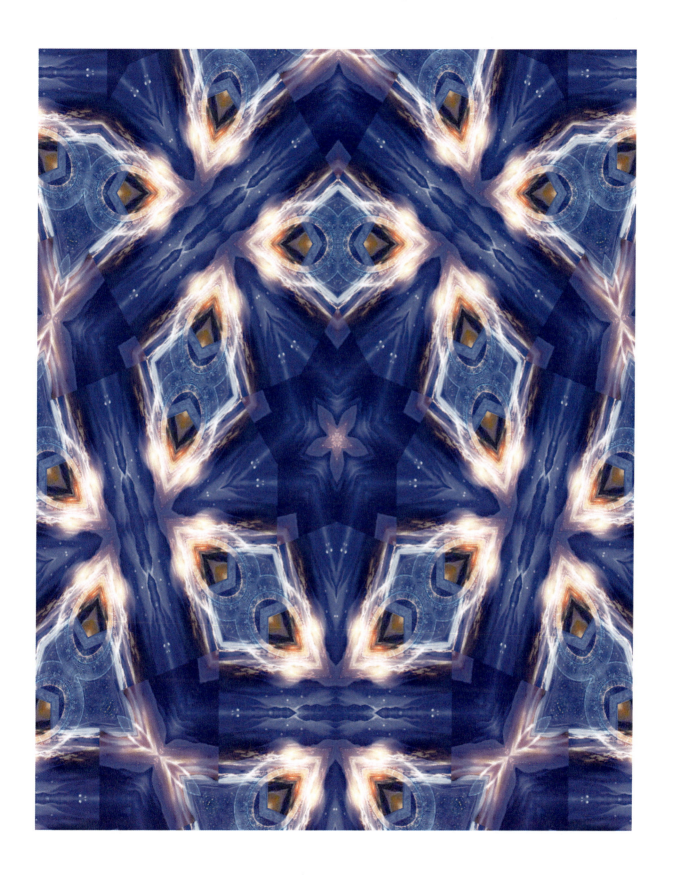

Light Portal Healing Grid 13

Light Portal Healing Grid 14 (Atlantean Language)

Atlantis: The Language of the Atlanteans

It is fascinating and informative to contemplate how our Atlantean ancestors developed linguistically alongside their physical and cultural evolution. As we learn more we may find ourselves wondering what language did the Atlanteans speak? The Atlantean language was vibrational, an energetic language that evolved from a deep spiritual knowing. The language included telepathy, and powerful sound vocalizations later depicted as pictographs and symbols which became a written language. The language was much different from the type of language that we focus on today. Contemplating the Atlantean language may lead to us looking at language in general in a deeper way. We will look to the thinkers and channels to recall their research and memories about the language of Atlantis. Most consider the language as a highly spiritually based language that aimed to help the Atlanteans live and create with clarity and ease. The language changed as the Atlanteans changed and the Earth changed. We may experience some of the language through channelings, Atlantean light language, as well as by looking at the languages of the more recent ancient civilizations that preceded Atlantis.

The Origins and Evolution of the Atlantean Language

Edgar Cayce on the Atlantean Language

The Atlanteans were not like the people of today, they were much closer to being spiritual in form and gradually became more physically dense as they evolved. The early Atlanteans were fully connected to source consciousness and so they possessed a deeply spiritual perspective as well as abilities that played a huge role in the formation of their language and the great civilization of Atlantis.

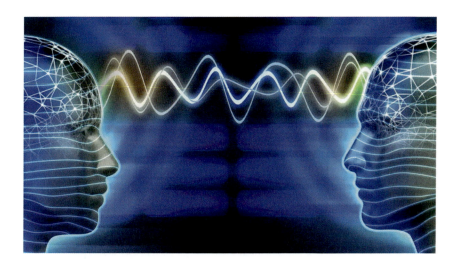

The Atlanteans existed in a very different consciousness, and they could communicate with each other telepathically. The Atlantean's deep connection to source energy and their knowledge of the truth of oneness allowed them to communicate via telepathy. The form of telepathy was initially not formed of specific mental words but rather specific energetic vibrations. As the

Atlanteans evolved to become more physically focused they developed spoken and written Atlantean language which was made up of pictographs. From the pictographs (pictures as a symbol for a word or a phrase) they developed logographs (characters representing words or phrases) and symbols (characters that represent something else) that were associated with specific sounds and words. This language is said to have been used worldwide towards the end times of Atlantis and was spoken in various dialects.

Atlantean Written Language Alphabet and Number System

Rudolf Steiner on the Atlantean Language

To more fully grasp this perspective on the development of the Atlantean language we can start with a small mention of the beings who preceded the first Atlanteans. Those who were called the Lemurian beings. They were highly spiritual beings that utilized telepathy, they were more ethereal than physical in form. The early Atlanteans were similar to these beings in some ways, they were more physical than the Lemurians but they were still quite etheric. Atlanteans developed the faculty of memory. Language was a key part of this development of memory in order to preserve and communicate with words or sounds their past experiences and knowings. Language was a way to externalize the internal world and to describe the outer world. Steiner described the Atanteans as being more ethereal than modern humans. Atlanteans, especially early Atlanteans had a deep connection with nature and so their language encompassed this innate power. Words were naming but also curative and directive. The magic power of words was a natural and tangible function for the Atlanteans. The language was "curative, they could advance the growth of plants, tame the rage of animals and perform other similar functions". The Atlantean language was considered as powerful and sacred; they treated language as a natural gift and power that they knew to use responsibly. As the Atlanteans evolved they became more ambitious and more interested in personal recognition this eventually led to many Atlanteans misusing their natural powers for selfish gain which caused imbalances. This is what led to the development of the faculty of thought in late Atlantean sub-races. Thought was intended to be a method of inner reflection. To think before speaking things into reality, and to keep selfish actions in check. The natural consequences of the development of thought caused the Atlanteans to lose some of their natural powers. This may well be how our ancestors began losing some of the original connections and understanding of the power of sound and words that originated from the Atlantean language.

Matias De Stefano on the Atlantean Language

The early Atlanteans had a clear memory and experience of the nature of the universe, the deep interconnection of everything. The knowing that God, the Divine was expressed in all of nature including ourselves. A deep knowledge of vibration, energy, and matter. Their innate knowledge is reflected in sacred geometry. The language of Atlanteans is considered as a vibratory language, "we as humans found out that words were not only something to communicate but also to transcend and transmit information, thoughts, dreams, concepts that cannot be seen, and emotions that cannot be expressed." The active intergalactic knowledge within the hybrid beings of Atlantis led to the development of a language that involved root sound vibrations that are reflected within the sacred geometry of the flower of life and the universe. The language was a vibratory tool to 'say the names of god'. The Atlantean language allowed them to remember and create through the instruction of sound, frequency, and vibration which could manifest powerful energetics for healing and protection in the body, mind and soul. The way to reflect on their knowledge was through the sound vibration or words. The language that developed was beyond just the function of communicating but it was used to intentionally create. The Atlantean language arose naturally from the rhythm of life and information represented within the patterns of the sacred geometry of the flower of life. The Atlantean language arose from the vibrations of inhalation, contemplation, and expression which allowed them to breathe creation to life through sound vibrations. The act of breathing was very important to the Atlantean's way of understanding and embodying God and they utilized language to express this so they had been connected to Christ consciousness and universal consciousness. Each of the aspects of the breathing process and the division or growth of the first 3 spheres within the flower of life was ascribed to a sound vibration:

- Ham which was related to inspiration and ideas
- Het which was about seeing everything within our ability
- Hum which is the realization that it is possible to do it.

This sound or breath of Ham, Het, and Hum together can be likened to the primordial Aum vibration that we see in many forms throughout many cultures till today. The next stage of geometric growth within the flower of life is known as the seed of life and it includes 9 aspects that informed the next 9 sound vibrations within the Atlantean language. These 9 vibrations are related to each of the 9 dimensions and are referred to by Matias as the Wanim. The language that developed contained energetic information and activation in the form of sound that was used to create an experience of oneness. By the latter years of Atlantis and during the start of the civilizations that succeeded Atlantis such as the Egyptians, a highly powerful language was passed down. This language was thought to the young to be used with great respect and importance. The Atlanteans were well aware of the power of sound vibration and language was used for its full power. Powerful sound vibrations were used to instruct and create reality. The Atlantean language was a result of the mixing of natural Earth DNA from humans and the DNA of star beings. The combination of inherent knowledge within the blood of Atlanteans led to the expression and development of the vibrational language that could put into words, sound, and spiritual embodiment the knowing that god is within every being. Through vibrational sound frequencies and acoustics the Atlanteans could levitate objects and even change solid matter into other elements or states of existence.

What is Atlantean Light Language?

In our present time, we may have come across the term Atlantis light language. Now that we have more ideas and understanding of the way that language was used in Atlantis; which is very different from the common ways of how we utilize language today. The experience of Atlantean light language may activate some remembrance or experiences of language as a powerful energy instead of just communication and naming of the physical. Light language can be understood as the channeled sound frequencies received by entering a nonlinear or meditative state. Channels or anyone willing to be a channel can tap into the collective consciousness that transcends time and space. We can tune into specific timelines or frequencies of Atlantean consciousness. Listening to, or channeling light language can have emotional and somatic effects on you or even an energetic or knowledge activation. Light language can align you energetically to the frequencies within the sound vibrations that make up the light language.

The Atlantean Pictorial Alphabet

The Atlantean language eventually included an alphabet of pictures and symbols that can be likened to what we know as hieroglyphics. When we consider the theories on Atlantis that share how Atlanteans may have migrated or colonized other areas of the world that became some of the ancient civilizations that we know more about such as the Egyptians and Mayans.

The Hieroglyphs of Atlantis probably resembled those of later Egypt. These civilizations are said to have inherited knowledge from Atlantis which is reflected in the megalithic structures and mythologies. When we look at the language of these civilizations both Egyptian and Mayan peoples used hieroglyphics as part of representing their language. Some researchers believe that there are similarities between the Egyptian and Mayan hieroglyphs as well as the phonetic alphabet which could stem back to the language originating from Atlantis. Egyptians credited their hieroglyphic written record of language to the gods. These gods could very well be their Atlantean ancestors who were considered to be godlike beings in many ways. To learn more about the details of this theory which actually traces back the development of the alphabet through time to originating from Atlantis, look to the work of Ignatius Donnelly in Chapter 7: The Origin of our Alphabet in his book Atlantis: The Antediluvian World.

The Atlanteans Communicated Memory and Knowledge

Although the Atlanteans were part of our ancestry they were much different than us in many ways; the physical Earth at the time was different, and their bodies were different, their way of perceiving reality and abilities were different from our understanding as modern humans. We can then deduce that their way of communicating was different than what we consider as language. The Atlanteans have a deeper knowledge of the power of words to create. The root sounds or vibrations were vocalized with a deep knowledge of the power of vibration. The language of Atlanteans was, especially in its early stages, more energetic than that of our mainstream modern-day focus on words. It was a language that held memory and knowledge in a way that the information could be preserved and passed down. We define language as a set system of communication. The Atlanteans had a way of communicating fundamental knowledge. The power of this knowledge was reflected in the very expression of the language itself, being energetic and vibratory with facets of telepathic communication. The language was not merely for communication it was used to tangibly instruct reality and many recall that in its prime the Atlantean civilization was deeply interconnected and thriving. There had been a language called Solex-Mal which was the original tongue that was once spoken on Earth by all people and it is still used by the inhabitants of other worlds in outer space. It is a symbolic, pictographic language. Solex means Solar, and Mal means Tongue. The Atlanteans had a portion of this language in their dialects and in written aspects of their figurative writings.

Creating sacred geometry in the Atlantean written language is part of learning how to create a sequence of healing nodes and vibrationally tuning into the frequencies of the healing codes that are found in the Atlantean language. Each healing node in the language has its specific tuning frequency coded for emotional healing, physical healing, soul healing, and quantum level healing on the higher dimensions. As well coding nodes can be used to create protection and for manifesting positive things in people's realities.

Information By: **Everet Dee – Mysteriumacademy**

sovereign integral

What was the Language of Atlantis & Lemuria?

Question: Did Lemuria and/or Atlantis have a written language? Can it be deciphered now? What language is most similar?

Answer: This is a good question and one that will help all of us regain a level of consciousness we once had—we should say, our souls had, for our personalities never had this level of consciousness. In answering your question, we are using Edgar Cayce's information from four principal readings: 364-10, 378-13, 378-14, and 2329-3, but also bits from the entire 364 series, the so-called "Atlantis Series."

We must understand that Lemuria was a very, very ancient time, literally millions of years ago, and Lemurians were not physical until the very last stages of their push into matter, roughly a few centuries. Atlantis, on the other hand, was a much closer period that lasted from 210,000 BC to 10,014 BC. And it is helpful if we divide Atlantis into three periods: the early formative centuries, the middle struggling centuries of increasing self-awareness resulting in rising selfishness, and then the final migration period as Atlantis sank in stages.

In the early period, Lemurians and Atlanteans were not like the people of today. Back then, you and I (our souls) would have been pure minds and spirits without physical bodies. And, importantly, we (our minds and spirits) were still connected to the Great Spirit and the Universal Consciousness of our Creator. We lived in conscious cooperation with our Creator, and possessed "all the attributes of the spiritual or unseen forces," giving us many abilities that we do not actively use today (they are now latent within us). Therefore, we did not use language the way we do today. The Cayce material teaches us that back then we were profoundly psychic. And when he was asked, "Give in detail of the psychic powers he [a reincarnated Atlantean] developed at that time [of Atlantis]?" Cayce replied, "This would almost be impossible." (378-13) Then Cayce attempted to explain that during our present "material age," we could hardly comprehend the oneness of consciousness among the Children of God and their Creator. In another reading he adds, "Individuals in the beginning were more of thought forms than individual entities with personalities as seen in the present..." (364-10) Can we today conceive of ourselves as minds without bodies? To a small degree, Edgar Cayce could be an example of an Atlantean, for even in his normal conscious state, he could know what you were thinking and had been doing. Telepathy was the means of communication back then, not sounds using vocal cords. But even this example can be misunderstood, because we today think of telepathy as "hearing" words in thought, but there were no words. As we Children of God, or "Morning Stars" as the book of Job referred to us, pushed our minds deeper and deeper into matter (this third dimensional plane), we became more individualized, and our expansive consciousness was narrowed into this world of form and physicality. When we were finally "out of Spirit, out of the ability to have all the attributes of the spiritual or unseen forces..." (364-10) and more fully in matter, then we moved toward writing and speaking. Language began as pictograms and pictographs, a language in which ideas are transmitted by drawing images, and these images are symbols representing a concept, object, activity, place, and the like—a picture being "worth a thousand words." For example, today if we saw a sign with an airplane and an arrow on it, we'd know, without words, that it shows the way to the airport. From pictographs developed logographs with increasing phonetics, symbols moving to sounds—mostly as a result of spoken language. This required vocal cords, and we were now in physical bodies, though Cayce states that bodies then were not as dense as ours today. Hieroglyphs are both pictographs and logographs. For example, the name "Ramses" is composed of pictographs of Ra (Sun god) and mess ("to be born"), meaning "he who is born of Ra." (See illustration.) But these symbols are also sounds, thus the phonetic name, which was originally spelled Ramesses, later simplified to Ramses. Cayce's readings indicate that the latter stages of Lemuria and Atlantis was a time when the whole world spoke one language, a time prior to the Tower of Babel legend in the Bible: "the understandings were of one tongue! There had not been as yet the divisions of tongues in this...Atlantean...land" (294-148) Therefore, we could assume that the three sets of Atlantis records are in the same language. In one reading, Cayce indicated that the Atlanteans had a slightly different dialect of the worldwide language: "...translations to the various dialects..." (852-12)

In another reading (2329-3), he actually stated that there are 32 plates or tablets— "records made by the entity itself," that are preserved in the Egyptian hall of records. He said that these tablets would require interpretation, and that this interpretation would take some time. It is likely that the glyphs on these tablets are a precursor to hieroglyphics, and therefore we should be able to decipher them. The Atlantean language was connected to expressing thought forms and thought transference from the natural world and the energies from the Earth so they used spirals, zigzag lines, etc. in their written communication and later on developed a more modern alphabet system that was used in writing, reading, astronomy and mathematics. Atlanteans were taught thought transference techniques as well as how to telepathically communicate with each other, animals, the Earth itself, they would meditate with relaxation breath work, breathing deeply in order to reach spiritual awareness and would listen to low pitched rhythmic sounds to raise their energetic frequencies so that they could connect with everything in the universe with their thought consciousness abilities. Many of the Atlanteans had learned astrology, prophecy, mind reading, dream interpretation, thought transference, and the use of thought projection to create material objects. Students learned to communicate with the spiritual world for advice and assistance in all affairs. They were encouraged to spend time with their natural surroundings, talking with flowers, making friends with birds, small animals, sensing that stones and rocks are alive and filled with tiny, rapidly moving particles, and exploring additional complex secrets of the world around them.

Information By: **John Van Auken – Edgarcayce**

Light Portal Healing Grid 15 (Atlantean Language)

If something physical is hurting like the neck, back, as well as hand pain or other types of pain in the body, to facilitate healing you would put your hands over the grid and focus your mind on the blue, purple, pink, and white healing energy of the Atlantean symbols to direct the healing energy frequency towards what hurts to heal it with these color frequencies. With the healing of the Atlantean energetics feel the pain dissipating and being completely healed and energized.

Light Portal Healing Grid 16 (Atlantean Language)

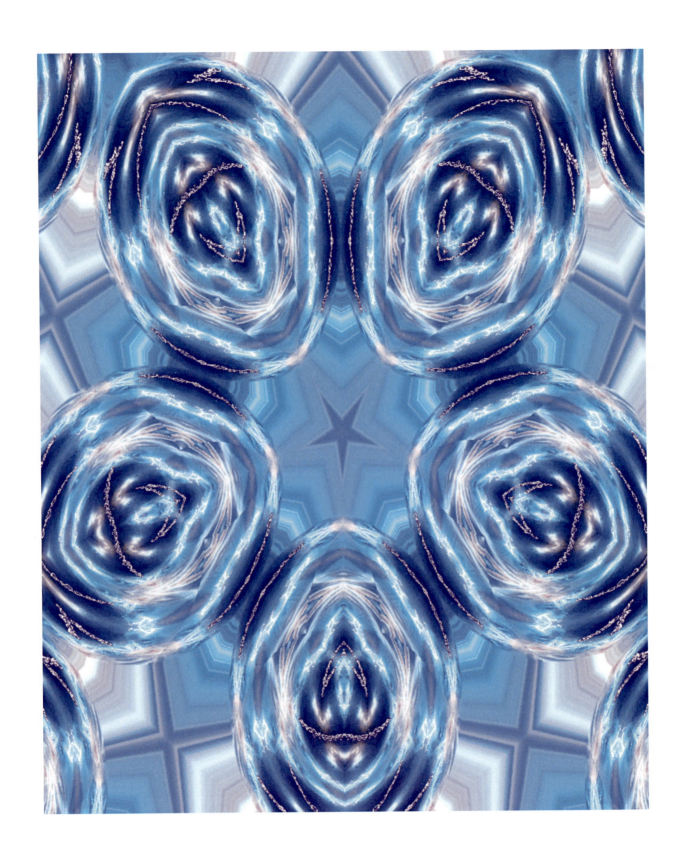

Light Portal Healing Grid 17 (Atlantean Language)

Light Portal Healing Grid 18 (Atlantean Language)

Light Portal Healing Grid 19 (Atlantean Language)

Light Portal Healing Grid 20 (Atlantean Language)

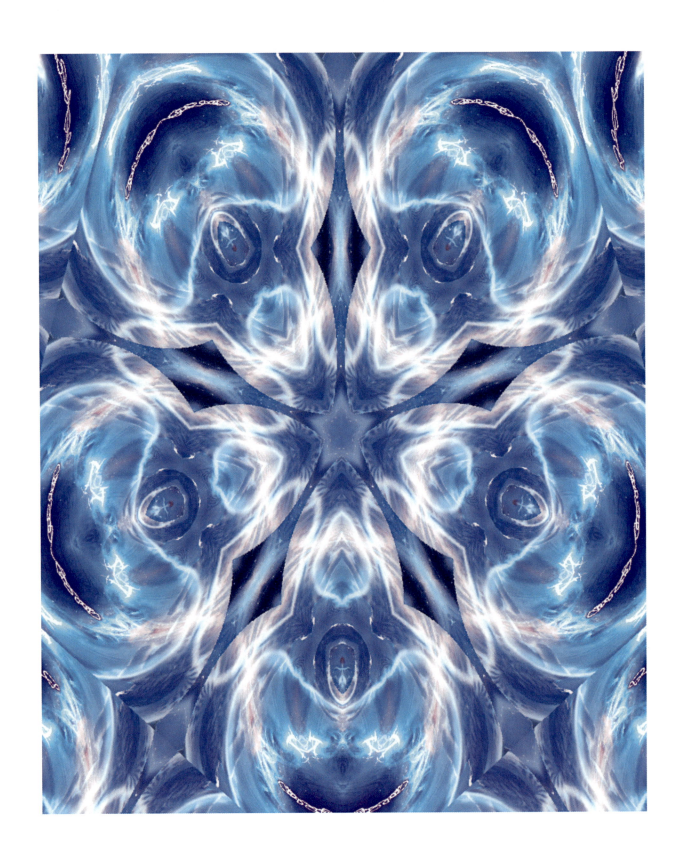

Light Portal Healing Grid 21 (Atlantean Language)

Light Portal Healing Grid 22

Light Portal Healing Grid 23

Light Portal Healing Grid 24

123

Light Portal Healing Grid 25

Light Portal Healing Grid 26

Light Portal Healing Grid 27

Light Portal Healing Grid 28

Light Portal Healing Grid 29

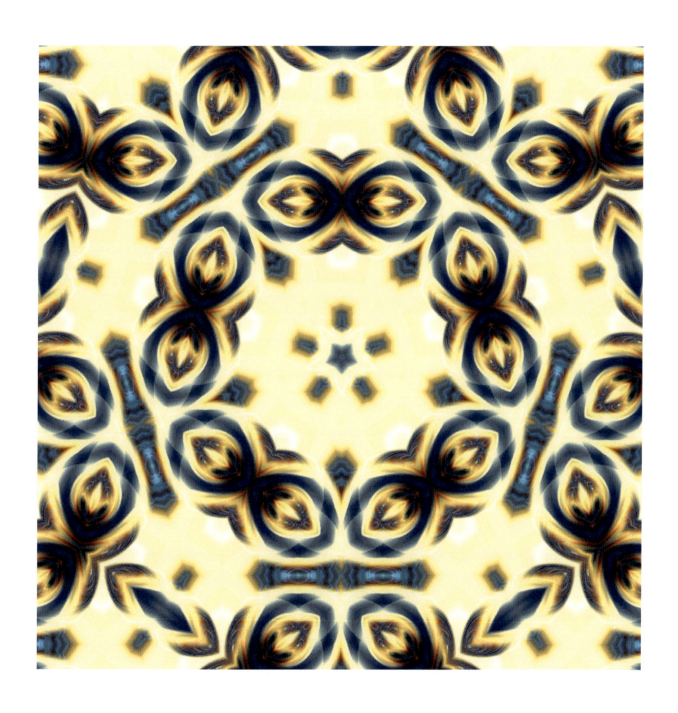

Light Portal Healing Grid 30

Solar Eclipse Portal Healing Grids

Solar eclipses are an ideal time for ritual, meditation, and internal clearing. Eclipses usually come in pairs, and the space between them is a powerful vortex time of transformation.

During Solar Eclipses the Moon is directly between the Earth and Sun (known as a conjunction between the Sun and the Moon). So during this brief time the Moon can "block out" the Sun, temporarily turning off the lights, if you will. We have a finite focus as human beings, and it's natural to concentrate on what's in front of us. At times, this can limit our perspectives on the world, and even cause us to miss out on opportunities. With the frequency energies of the Solar Eclipses they might snatch away the familiar temporarily, forcing us to consider options we would never otherwise explore. Although this can cause temporary upheaval, eclipses are "cruel to be kind." Major growth can happen during these cosmic power outages. This is when we should leap into new (and generally improved) terrain, even if we feel forced there by circumstance.

The major solar eclipses focus on healing deep wounds in your soul, represented by Chiron alongside the solar eclipse. It may be an old or new wound affecting your body, mind or spirit. Growing pains due to challenging aspects coming from Jupiter and Saturn are relieved by the recuperative and evolving power of Pluto. Freedom from pain allows for a spiritual transformation, the evolution of your soul.

Solar Eclipse Portal Healing Grid 1

Solar Eclipse Portal Healing Grid 2

Solar Eclipse Portal Healing Grid 3

Solar Eclipse Portal Healing Grid 4

Solar Eclipse Portal Healing Grid 5

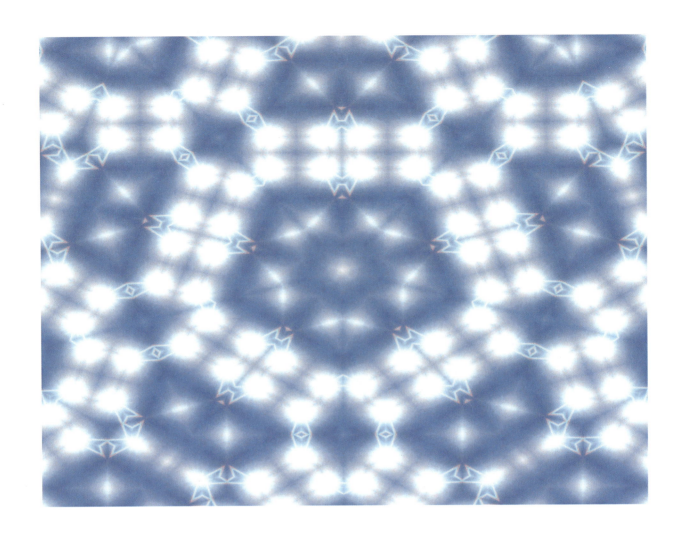

Solar Eclipse Portal Healing Grid 6

Solar Eclipse Portal Healing Grid 7

Solar Eclipse Portal Healing Grid 8

Solar Eclipse Portal Healing Grid 9

Solar Eclipse Portal Healing Grid 10

Solar Eclipse Portal Healing Grid 11

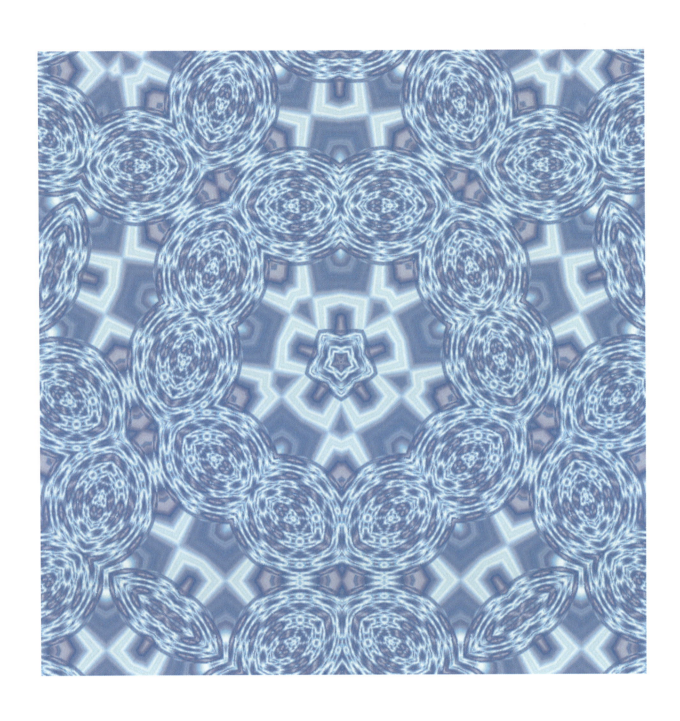

Solar Eclipse Portal Healing Grid 12

Diamond Sun DNA Code Aquaelle Transmissions

The organic angelic human DNA, also known as Diamond Sun DNA is built upon gender pairs in which the mother's lineage generates the genetic imprint for the magnetic particle base, and the father's lineage generates the genetic imprint for the electrical anti-particle base. The unification of Gender Principle is inherently built into the original angelic human DNA which is designed to naturally evolve into the Christos-Sophia pattern of divine hierogamic union. Human DNA is composed of tiny sparks of crystalline frequencies that are arranged in electromagnetic light sparks that are bound by magnetism which forms into a crystalline matrix. The instruction set for the Diamond Sun DNA is held within the Crystal Body which must be activated through the opening heart center. As a result of NAA invasion and genetic mutations, very few humans on Earth held the entire silicate matrix instruction set in their DNA. Many distortions were being caused by the lunar matrix, artificial magnetic fields and assorted implants of alien machinery which generated damage in the Crystal Body. However, this is now changing during the planetary ascension stages of restoration of the solar feminine principle, as the organic magnetism resets and allows the Holy Mother lineages to generate the correct sound body imprints for the magnetic particle base, including corrections to upgrade the mitochondria and chromosomes.

Historically, the Keepers of the Flame and the genetic descendants of Yeshua from the Aquaelle matrix carried the krystal gene code for humanity which was essentially the silicate matrix imprint that held all twelve strands of DNA that was capable of biological ascension. Aquaelle is directly related to the daughter of Christ bloodlines that incarnated on earth from Andromeda, and this is also an embodiment coding potential for bringing forth the Diamond Sun body, which influences the potential of both male and female unification, hierogamic union. The progeny of Aquaelle was brought through the human tribes that became the male and female twins known as White Buffalo Calf Woman and White Navajo as the direct descendants protecting the mother solar twin coding on the Earth. The 12 strand DNA template is the original human genome first seeded upon Tara that was destroyed during the Fall, and was secretly being protected by certain tribes in the Earth grids during the Dark Age.

The 12 DNA strands of the core Diamond Sun DNA template each correspond to a dimensional band within the human lightbody. The DNA is the primary structure which consciousness translates into manifestation within a biological form. Each of the 12 DNA strands hold 24 seed codes and a total of 144 fire letters which connect to the subharmonic frequencies that make up each dimension. When these seed codes and fire letters are activated, this allows for dimensional expansion of the consciousness perception. Within each of the 12 strands of DNA are 12 base codes which control DNA's magnetic force, and the 12 acceleration codes which control the DNA's electrical force.

The male electrical codes and female magnetic codes are designed to plug into each other which accelerates the body's frequency rate to merge into harmonious electromagnetic balance, which further ignites blood crystals that accelerate various biological processes to build out the lightbody. During the intense phase of planetary plasma activations, the 12 strand Diamond Sun DNA base codes, acceleration codes, crystal seals and fire letters are being transmitted throughout the planetary grid network. Those that open their higher hearts during monadic integration with unconditional love, compassion and empathy, desiring to spiritually evolve will connect with their Crystal Body. The Crystal Body is being upgraded through the return of the Emerald Order, and thus will finally be able to transmit the necessary DNA seed codes to reassemble and activate a range of the Diamond Sun DNA templates and plasma lightbody codes in humanity.

Information By: **Lisa Renee – Ascension Glossary**

Light Code Activation and Transmission

Light Codes

What are light codes?

Light codes are your personal frequency transmissions, your cosmic fingerprints. Every living being is encoded at birth with a specific set of codes that they are to transmit during their lifetime; it is the goal of many lightworkers to understand their codes as well as their methods of transmission.

Light codes are connected to light languages, they can feel the same but the vibration can also feel different since when your soul light codes activate they start to connect you with your light language heritage then you begin to energetically match up which light codes create the activations for which light languages that the codes belong to.

We transmit light codes by embodying the light field crystalline source that is within our souls and bodies we can expand the light codes from within the core of our soul self thereby going outward to the rest of the body and its auric fields to restore our original DNA blueprint and heal the body, mind, and the soul as a whole instead of in various parts.

Light codes are interconnected by energy and frequency on the quantum level to facilitate healing, astral as well as inter-dimensional travel and do energy work on the quantum levels for whole healing modalities.

Expressing Light Codes

You express a light code, for example, when you look into another person's eyes, when you pray or bless another person, and when you gift things to another person that transmits the light code frequencies for connecting on a soul level with someone else to help them elevate their life frequencies.

"Your words are only 10% of the energy you transmit. Everything else is code."

"If you want to experience profound healing on multiple levels, working with codes is an excellent place to begin. Light codes can be activated within the soul and the body to facilitate healing yourself, healing others, healing our planet, which needs our loving attention more now than ever.

All beings have light codes – but not all beings remember or have access to theirs. When light codes are activated it helps us to remember who we are as energetic beings and to become aware of your greater purpose. You came to this life to have these energetic experiences; you wanted free will, you wanted to see what your gifts were, and you sought the chance to engage powerfully with your gifts in this lifetime. Light codes and light languages elevate your life force frequencies to know how to use your unique light codes in order to unlock new levels of wisdom so that you can remember who you are on the light spectrum and become aware of your greater purpose. You will be able to access your codes on demand and then if you desire, you can channel a set of symbols for your unique codes or find other interesting ways to communicate them. After all, most cosmic languages are symbol-based and are not spoken.

The most powerful languages in the world are those not spoken;

- Your gemstones are languages
- Your essential oils are languages
- Your body is a form of language
- Your kiss and your touch are languages
- And the way you smell is a language

You are communicating all the time on the light and source field of your higher creation; light codes can make your constant communication more intentional.

Light codes are the keys to our freedom as third dimensional beings. They allow you to see your problems from a different perspective. When you are dancing on the dance floor of life, you have no perspective on what is happening; when you elevate, lift up, and rise above, accessing more subtle methods of communication, you gain perspective, clarity, and power. When you activate your light codes you will use them for a lifetime, and you will learn how your own soul gifts can be used to help the world.

Information By: **Sagegoddess**

12 Stranded DNA & 24 Seed Codes Activations Coming Online Through the Solar Eclipse

The solar eclipse that had happened on October 14, 2023 had manifested the 12 stranded DNA and the 24 seed codes, these manifestations showed themselves in the form of a crescent moon being overlapped over the sun and the Star of David in brilliant rays of light streaming in the sky, this was shown in one of the solar eclipse images from Mexico. There were powerful sun codes, fire codes being revealed within the image that allow us to see the structures of the 12 stranded DNA and the 24 seed codes taking us back into the original Blueprint of healing the soul within as it goes outwards with the light codes on this healing journey to heal the auric fields, meridians, as it activates the golden spiral of the kundalini awakening energies spinning within the body, mind, and soul creating complete system upgrades on the light fields for whole healing instead of just parts of healing for humans. It is us moving upwards on the higher frequency consciousness of existence into 5D frequencies and densities from 3D bodies merging with 5D energies thereby making our bodies lighter with the crystalline and diamond light code activations for DNA so our bodies are aligned with 5D existence on 5D New Earth. It's not leaving our bodies or the planet but merging into 5D energy fields on planetary and physical evolution in this world. We are ascending upwards back into higher consciousness DNA upgrades of 5D and above not ascending/descending downwards staying at 3D level capacity. This is part of our ascension on the evolutionary scale in current realities.

Sacred Geometry Healing and Protection Grids

Healing and protection grids can be made of sacred geometry symbols that have positively encoded frequencies to create a purpose of healing for the body, mind and the soul where whole healing happens on the quantum scale. As well the symbols in the grids can set intent for creating positive manifestation for accomplishing ones goals and creating successful outcomes in life. The purpose of the grids starts with one's energetic intent for how the grids will be programmed for what type of a creative outcome will occur with this intent like for example having home protection, healing, success, happiness, balancing and grounding during meditation, etc.

The healing and protection grids can be made in the form of digital art that can be put as a screen cover, print, grid, protection on devices to block negative energies and have a portable functionality where they can be on someone's computer, cell phone and act as part of the healing or protection process wherever you go.

Sacred geometry that has a positive intent and is imbued with healing colors, symbols thereby will act as protective frequencies for good health and wellbeing. People can often feel the energies of wellbeing and good vibration from grids that uplift the soul on its evolutionary path of self-discovery for creative manifestation in accomplishing something extraordinary on the journey of life creation. The grids help you to connect with the aspects of your intuitive self and to guide you to reach your path of exploring who you are meant to be in reaching your purpose and mission in life. As well the grids can have patterns or vibrational designs that connect your soul to something that has meaning to you and represents a special point in your life that is significant in how it can open your world to create profound opportunities and the ability to improve things for you to remove blockages or whatever it was that was stopping you from moving forward with your highest wellbeing where positive change should be occurring. It is a chance to explore the aspects of yourself in understanding who you are and how you grow as a soul being.

10 Ancient Sites That Might Be Stargates, Portals and Wormholes

Many ancient cultures speak of portals to other worlds and gateways to star systems where their "creators" reside. These teachings are considered to be part of myths and legends. However, recent declassified FBI files have stated that our Earth has been visited by beings from other dimensions and planets. NASA has announced that "portals" do indeed appear to be hidden within the Earth's magnetic field, making some wonder if the legends of stargates, portals and wormholes may have some degree of truth to them.

10 Gate of the Gods (Amaru Muru Stargate), Hayu Marca, Peru

In 1996, the Amaru Muru Stargate with a giant door and carved lock entrance was discovered by Jose Luis Delgado Mamani while he was trying to learn the layout of the area for a job he had recently taken as a tour guide in Peru. The "Gate of the Gods" at Hayu Marca in Peru is said by native tribes to have once acted as a "gateway to the land of the Gods." Mamani even claims that he had dreams of the doorway for years before he had accidentally found it. In his dream, Mamani stated that the pathway leading to the doorway was made of pink marble, and had also witnessed a smaller door that was open with a "brilliant blue light coming from what looked like a shimmering tunnel." The "doorway" is actually two doorways, almost in a "T" shape. The larger doorway measures seven meters wide and seven meters high (22 ft. by 22 ft.) while the smaller one stands two meters high (6.5 ft.) in the middle of the base. Legends state that the larger door is for the gods, themselves. The smaller door is for mortals to pass through, and some heroic mortals did, becoming immortal themselves to live among the gods. One legend of a mortal passing through the doorway appears to lend a little credibility to Mamani's alleged dream. The story says that when Spanish explorers arrived in Peru in the 16th century, looting Inca riches as they went, an Incan priest named Amaru Muru fled his temple with a valuable golden sun disk— "The Key of the Gods of the Seven Rays." Amaru Muru found the doorway and saw it was guarded by Shaman priests. He presented to them the golden sun disk, and following a ritual performed by the priests, the smaller doorway opened. Behind it was a tunnel that shone with great blue light. Amaru Muru passed into the doorway, left the disk with the Shaman priests, and vanished from Earth to the land of the gods. Interestingly, investigators did discover a small, round, indention in the rock on the right hand column of the smaller doorway. The examinations led them to believe that should a disk shaped object be "inserted" into the indention, it would be held in place by the surrounding rock. The Amaru Muru monument is located near Lake Titicaca.

9 Abu Ghurab, Egypt, the Place of the Gods

The Abu Sir Pyramids, site of Abu Ghurab, has claimed to be one of the oldest sites on the planet. Within Abu Ghurab, lies an ancient platform made of alabaster (Egyptian crystal) and is said to be in tune with the "vibration" of Earth. It can also "open the senses" in order for a person to communicate and "be one" with higher, sacred energies of the Universe. Essentially, it is a stargate and the sacred energies were the Neters (gods).

Interestingly, legends of their communication and way of travel between their world and ours almost mirrors the legends of the Cherokee Native Americans. The Cherokee tell of how "thought beings"—who are formless—would travel on a "wave of sound" from their home in the Pleiades Star System to Earth.

As the legends of Abu Ghurab point to it being a stargate, there are also signs of what some would perceive to be advanced technology having been used to create the site. One example is the perfectly precise circular markings that have been drilled into the alabaster.

8 Ancient Stone Arrangement in Lake Michigan

In 2007, while searching for the remains of shipwrecks, scientists discovered a stone structure 12 meters (40 ft.) below the surface of Lake Michigan. Thought to be 9,000 years old, the structure has been dubbed Michigan's equivalent of Stonehenge. The discovery was made by professor of underwater archaeology at Northwestern Michigan University, Mark Holley, and his colleague, Brian Abbott. One thing of particular interest was a carving on one of the stones of a mastodon— which is believed to have become extinct 10,000 years ago—a possible indication of the structure's age.

The location of the site has been kept secret, at least for now. This is part of an agreement with the local Native American tribes who wish to keep the amount of visitors to a minimum. While a lot of mainstream scientists are skeptical about the age of the site, and if it even has any relevance, many believe that it is the remains of a stargate or wormhole. The site has also claimed several bizarre disappearances and gained the title of "The Michigan Triangle."

In 1891, a schooner named the Thomas Hume vanished into thin air along with all seven of its crew while sailing on the lake. In 1921, the 11 people who were aboard the Rosa Belle disappeared without a trace, but their boat was found floating lifelessly in the water. In 1937, while on board the O.M. McFarland as it made its way along Lake Michigan, Captain Donner retired to his quarters to get some much needed rest after a long shift on deck. Three hours later, the second mate went to wake his captain. Finding the door locked from the inside, and with no response from the captain, he eventually broke down the door to the room. With the captain's quarters empty and with all the windows locked shut, Captain Donner had simply vanished.

7 Stonehenge, Wiltshire, England

One of the most well-known structures on the planet, if only by name, is the ancient rock formation known as Stonehenge. It is also one of the most contested and debated sites in history, both as to when it was built and to what its true purpose might have been. Mainstream historians claim that the famous arrangement was built around 5,000 years ago, partly from bluestones that were quarried from a site 386 kilometers (240 miles) away. To some though, this notion is absurd.

Geologist Brian John states that there has been no evidence for this claim and no evidence that the alleged quarry even existed. It is said that when the first settlements were built in the area, 5,000 years ago, Stonehenge was already there and fully built. The ancient site is said to sit where 14 ley lines converge and some feel, along with other similar ancient sites, this essentially makes it an energy portal or stargate.

At least one incident in recent history may support this seemingly crazy theory. In August 1971, a group of hippies apparently disappeared at Stonehenge while trying to tap into the "vibrations" of the site. At around 2 o'clock in the morning, without any warning, lightning bolts suddenly struck and a severe storm was unleashed onto the area. According to the story, a policeman who happened to be on duty and in the area, recalls seeing a "blue light" coming from the stones – a local farmer also stated he saw this. Screams could be heard from the area. By the time the policeman had made his way to the site, all that remained was the odd tent peg from the reveler's tents and the damp remains of a campfire.

6 The Ancient Sumerian Stargate at the Euphrates River

There is a famous Sumerian seal that shows a Sumerian god appearing from a portal of his world into ours. The god appears to be on a staircase that is moving away from the person viewing the seal. On each side of the emerging god, there are strange shimmering columns of water. Another Sumerian artifact that claims to show evidence of stargates is that of Ninurta. Ninurta not only appears to be wearing a modern day wristwatch, but is also using his finger to press what appears to be a button on the wall of the gateway he is standing in.

Author Elizabeth Vegh has written several books on the ancient Sumerian gods and kings and their alleged use of stargates in ancient times. One of her main conclusions is that there is a stargate in the Euphrates River, and it has been buried and lost under the ruins of the Mesopotamian city of Eridu for thousands of years. Vegh also states that the biblical verse in Chapter 9 of the Book of Revelations speaks of this stargate. The verse reads, "(1) Then the fifth angel sounded his trumpet, and I saw a star that had fallen from heaven to earth, and it was given the key to the pit of the abyss. (2) The star opened the pit of the abyss, and smoke rose out of it like the smoke of a great furnace, and the sun and the air were darkened by the smoke from the pit. (3) And out of the smoke, locusts descended on the earth . . ."

Although most scholars would agree that the word "abyss" refers to a large body of water, Vegh argues that, as it's used in ancient texts, it is more likely to have a meaning more akin to that of a portal.

5 Tiahuanaco, Bolivia, 'Gate of the Sun'

Believed by some to be a portal to the land of the gods, the "Gate of the Sun" in Bolivia shares much of its legends with other similar sites in the Andes region. Tiahuanaco city is said to be one of the most important sites of ancient America, with legends stating that the Sun god, Viracocha, appeared in Tiahuanaco and made it "the place of creation"—the place he chose to start the human race.

Carved from one block of stone and thought to be 14,000 years old, the gateway displays what appears to be human beings with "rectangular helmets". This has led many researchers to state the purpose of the gate is indeed connected to something astronomical, although this is hotly debated. The top-middle of the arch features a carving of the supposed sun god and shows what looks to be rays of light appearing behind and forcing their way around all sides of the deities head.

Although it now stands upright, when it was found by European explorers in the mid-1800's, it was said to have been lying horizontally. It also appears to have a large crack to the top right of the arch. It is unknown how this happened.

4 Ranmasu Uyana Stargate, Sri Lanka

Carved on a massive piece of stone wall and mostly hidden between the boulders and cave systems of Ranmasu Uyana, it is thought to be what is believed to be a star map or star chart. The symbols carved on the rock are said to be a code that opens the star gate and allows the opener to travel from this world to other areas of the universe. Directly opposite the star map, are four stone seats or chairs.

The name of the star chart is Sakwala Chakraya, which is believed to mean "The rotating circle of the Universe." According to Sinhala interpretation, Sakwala means universe and Chakraya means a rotating circle or disc.

In many ancient Native American legends, stargates or portals were represented by rotating circles. Similar star maps have also been found in other ancient sites said to be stargates, such as the Abu Ghurab in Egypt and many more ancient sites in the Andes of South America. Yet, mainstream historians disregard the notion that the Sakwla Chakraya is a portal or stargate.

3 Abydos, Egypt

One of the oldest cities of Ancient Egypt, Abydos is perhaps one of the most important sites in Egyptology and certainly one of the most interesting. In particular, the Temple of Seti I appears to show hieroglyphs of modern flying machines, such as a helicopter, as well as what some would describe as a flying saucer.

Perhaps even more amazing is how a lot of the site was discovered. A lady named Dorothy Eady had claimed to be the reincarnation of an Egyptian peasant girl named Bentreshyt and was the secret lover of Pharaoh Seti. She had become pregnant with his child, but before he could learn of the pregnancy, the peasant girl took her own life. Now in the 20th century, Dorothy was able to transcribe ancient Egyptian texts and even knew where the archaeologists should dig to excavate the remains of the ancient city. She seemingly knew where everything was, such as where secret chambers were and the location of gardens that had long since been buried. By the time they discovered precisely where she said they would be, people very much believed she was genuine.

Strangely, people also witnessed Dorothy pressing on certain stones in the walls, as if she was expecting something to happen when she did so. It was as if she was trying to open a secret door or gateway. In fact, she had already spoken about these hidden doors that used to be there. In 2003, Michael Schratt, a military aerospace engineer, stated that Abydos did sit on a naturally occurring stargate. Even more controversially, that the US government was very much aware of this and had actually utilized it.

Was this what Eady was looking for when she was pressing stones in the walls? Aside from the unusual helicopter hieroglyphs, comparisons have been made to the paintings of Egyptian boats that were said to carry its passengers to the next world in the stars, being very similar to how modern day scientists would portray a wormhole, or at least the theory of one.

2 Gobekli Tepe, Turkey

Regarded as the oldest stone temple in the world, the Gobekli Tepe site features several rings of huge "T" shaped stone pillars, each engraved with a carving of an animal such as a lion or a sheep. Two of the pillars sit in the middle of these circles, almost creating an archway of sorts. The archway within these circles are said to be the remains of portals or stargates, which the ancient people who resided here used as a portal to the "sky world."

The "T" columns are very similar to the "Gate of the Gods" at Hayu Marca in Peru. Interestingly, the Inca people spoke of a connection to the people from the Pleiades star system, which is also T-shaped. Like other alleged portals, Gobekli Tepe is situated where two ley lines meet. Although the site was recorded as far back as the 1960's, it wasn't until the mid-90's when the T-Shaped pillars were discovered. As for its true age, estimations date it around 12,000 years old.

1 Sedona Vortexes and the 'Doorway of the Gods'

Sedona, a small town in Arizona was once known by the Native American tribes as Nawanda, and at one time, a most sacred city to them. It is said the Red Rocks of the deserts that surround the small town can create vortexes with the capability of transporting people to another realm or dimension. Native Americans believed these rocks were spiritually charged, while sounds emanating from them have been reported. In the mountains of Arizona, there have been claims made that these sites are part of the "Doorway of the gods"—which is a strange stone arch portal to another time and space.

In the 1950's, a local tribesman was aiding treasure hunters who were searching for gold in the mountains. He told them a story of his people, dating back to the 1800's, of three tribesmen who had discovered the archway while riding in the desert. The story goes that when one of them walked through, he simply disappeared. The other two, believing they had encroached on sacred land, fled the scene.

The helpful tribesman stated he had also seen a strange incident at the alleged doorway. While out in the desert, a sudden rain storm hit the area and turned the skies grey with clouds. As he turned to leave, he caught a glimpse of the archway, and saw that the skies through the arch were clear blue. He walked closer to it, seeing that the archway's image of the mountain range was the same and the only difference was the sky. However, he too, became scared, mounted his horse and returned home.

He told the treasure hunters that only his people knew of the stories. He had only spoke of it because they had shown him kindness and to serve as a warning to not walk through the archway should they come across it.

Information By: **Marcus Lowth – Listverse**

Earth's Natural Stargates

- 1D Stargate Sedona, Arizona 35° N, 111.8° W
- 1D Inner gate Cyprus 35.1264° N, 33.4299° E
- 2D Stargate Temple Mount 31.7781° N, 35.2360° E
- 2D Stargate Sarasota, Florida 27.3364° N, 82.5307° W - FPM
- 2D Inner gate Easter Island, Chile (Grual-Grail Point)
- 3D Stargate Bermuda Triangle 25° N, 71° W
- 3D Inner gate Johannesburg, South Africa 26.2041° S, 28.0473° E
- 4D Stargate Giza, Egypt 29.9753º N 31.1376º E
- 4D Inner gate Central Mexico, Aguascalientes 21.8853ºN, 102.2916º W
- 5D Stargate Machu Picchu 13.1631º S, 72.545º W
- 5D Inner Gate Vatican City 41.9029º N, 12.4534º E
- 6D Stargate Caucasus Mountains at Russia & Georgia border 42.639ºN, 44.155ºE
- 6D Inner gate Thar Desert at India & Pakistani border 27.47ºN, 70.6ºE
- 7D Stargate Lake Titicaca 15.9254º S, 69.3354º W
- 7D Inner gate Ionian Islands, city of Gaios on Paxos 39.2ºN, 20.18333º E
- 8D Stargate Xian, China 34.3416º N, 108.9398º E
- 8D Inner gate Lop Nur, border Tibet/China 40.1666º N, 90.5833º E
- 9D Stargate Tibet Autonomous Region, Bam Co Lake 31.25277778º N, 90.57861111º E
- 9D Inner gate Valley of the White Horse, Westbury England 51.26361111º N, 2.14694444ºW
- 10D Stargate Abadan, Iran 30.3ºN, 48.3º E

- 10D Inner gate Basrah, Iraq 30.5081ºN, 47.7835º E
- 11D Stargate Vale of Pewsey, Amesbury, Wiltshire, UK (Stonehenge) 51.1679º N, 1.763º W
- 11D Inner gate Ireland's Eye, Irish Sea 53.404608º N, 6.063344º W
- 11D Inner gate St. Ives Bay, Cornwall, UK 50.211º N, 5.48º W (Grual-Grail Point)
- 12D Stargate Monsegur, southern France 44.65º N, 0.0803º E
  As well there is another Stargate located at the Cucugnan Valley – Route Des Cathars, France

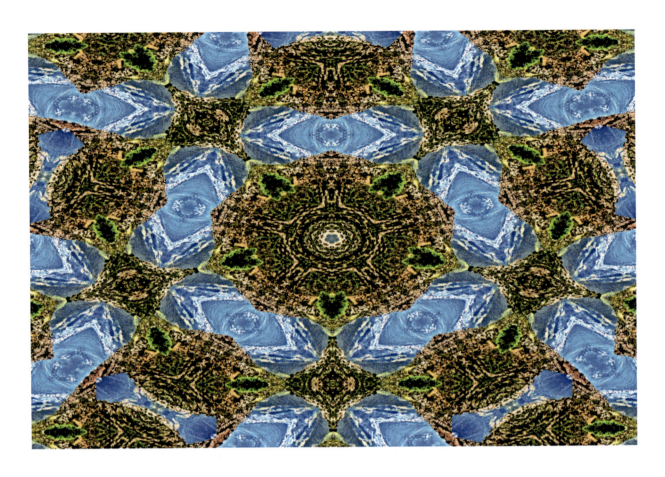

12D Inner gate Kauai 22.16444º N, 159.65722º W

Information By: **Lisa Renee – Ascension Glossary**

STARGATES

Planetary

- Monsegur & Kauai
- Vale of Pewsey & Eye Island
- Bam Tso & Westbury
- Abadan & Basra
- Xian & Lop Nur
- Moscow & Thar Desert
- Lake Titicaca & Paxos
- Machu Pichhu & Vatican
- Bermuda & Johannesberg
- Giza & Aquascalientes
- Sarasota & Easter Is
- Halley & Cyprus

Galactic

- Sun
- Nibiru
- Neptune
- Pluto
- Uranus
- Jupiter
- Saturn
- Maldak
- Earth
- Mars
- Venus
- Mercury

Universal

- LYRA Aramatena
- LYRA Aveyon Avalon
- ANDROMEDA Mirach
- LYRA Vega
- ORION Alnitak Mintaka
- SIRIUS B Procyon
- ARCTURUS Omega Centauri
- PLEIADES Alcyone
- Alpha Centauri
- NIBIRU
- Epsilon Eridani
- ORION Theta

Stargate Portals & Installations Worldwide

Worldwide Stargate Portals

Canada

Alberta:

- Banff: 4 Portals
- Calgary: 4 Portals
- British Columbia:
- Vancouver: 5 Portals

Ontario:

- Algonquin Park: 3 portals
- Barry's Bay: 2 Portals
- Barrie: 3 Portals
- Caledon: 1Portal
- Dwight: 3 Portal
- Green River: 6 Portals
- Huntsville: 4 Portals
- London: 2 Portals
- Markham: 30 Portals
- Port Perry: 10 Portals
- Ragged Falls: 10 Portals
- Temagami: 3 Portals
- Thornbury: 3 Portals
- Toronto: 30 Portals
- Uxbridge: 10 Portals
- Windsor: 4 portals

Quebec:

- Montreal: 5 Portals

USA

Arizona:

- Grand Canyon National Park: 2 Portals
- Flagg Staff: 1 Portal
- Oak Creek: 20 Portals

- Sedona: 10 Portals

Colorado:

- Arvada: 10 Portals
- Boulder: 30 Portals
- Crestone: 10 Portals
- Denver: 5 Portals
- Dillon: 1 Portal
- Estes Park: 2 Portals
- Gunbarrel: 6 Portals
- Longmont: 6 Portals
- Loveland: 5 portals
- Lyons: 10 Portals

Worldwide Stargate Portals

USA cont.:

Colorado:

- Niwot: 15 Portals
- Ouray: 2 Portals
- Rocky Mountain National Park: 3 Portals

Florida:

- Del Ray Beach: 3 Portals
- Hallandale Beach: 10 portals
- Hollywood Beach: 2 Portals
- Miami: 10 Portals
- Miami Beach: 2 Portals
- Orlando: 4 Portals

Massachusetts:

- Great Barrington: 5 Portals

New York:

- Catskills: 10 portals
- Mohegan Lake: 15 Portals
- Peekskill: 10 portals
- Saugerties: 4 Portals

- Manhattan: 10 Portals
- Wappinger Falls: 3 Portals

Long Island NY:

- East Hampton: 4 Portals
- Montauk: 4 Portals
- Long Beach: 4 Portals
- South Hampton: 2 portals

New Jersey:

- Newark: 3 portals

Pennsylvania:

- Pittsburgh: 10 Portals

Rhode Island:

- Providence: 6 Portals

China

- Guangzhou Shi-Guangdong
- University of Foreign Studies: 4 Portals

175

The Akashic Records: Everything You Need to Know about the Library of the Universe

The Akashic Records contain the entire history of every soul that ever existed. They hold the energetic record of your soul's journey through every lifetime since its inception at Source.

The information stored in the Akashic Records has enormous influence on your everyday life. It holds the key to understanding your soul's purpose, your relationships, your choices, your tendencies and belief systems as well as the reality that you create.

In this communication we answer the most frequently asked questions about the Akashic Records, drawing on our experience as an Akashic Record reader and an energy worker.

You will learn:

- What are the Akashic Records and where are they kept?
- What do the Akashic Records look like?
- How to access your Akashic Record?
- How to release karma from your past lives with the help of the Akashic Records?
- How to read the Akashic Records?

In a modern world run by innovative cloud-based and data-centric technologies, everything is within reach in one Google search through your smartphone, laptop and any other electronic devices. This gives us humans the capability to expand our knowledge in a variety of things, at least from the 3D reality perspective.

If you are one of those awakened souls who believe that you have a greater sense of purpose here on Earth, you know that learning about your mission is not something as easy as scanning through the Internet with a specific keyword search or phrase that creates a sentence. The truth is only by accessing your Akashic Records will you gain a profound understanding of your true sense of being.

What are the Akashic Records and where are they kept?

The Akashic Records are like a ledger or a recording of everything that is, has been and will be. Within the life experiences recorded are the karma and lessons you have accumulated throughout your lifetimes. Akashic Records belong to the 12th dimensions or frequency band called the Akashic Realm. Within that realm, there are three layers: the Akashic Records itself, the karmic field of energy, and the consciousness of the Akashic Records.

The Akashic Realm contains all the blocks we have gathered throughout our lifetimes, as terrestrial and Galactic beings. These are represented in the karmic realm. The terrestrial block contains records from the lifetimes here on Earth. However, some of us have lived a lifetime or a few as a member of different Galactic Races so there is also the Galactic block.

When you compare these two, the terrestrial block is twice the size of the galactic block because as human beings on Earth, we live through the greatest opportunity for soul evolution and as a result, gather the most amount of karma that separates us from our higher self. This creates a significant gap between us humans and the Galactic Races because in comparison, they are able to live a more balanced existence.

What do Akashic Records look like?

The first time we accessed the Akashic Records, we were able to utilize some help from the Pleiadians. These high vibrational Beings of Light sent their frequencies to us through a Merkabah or it can happen through the quantum vibrational fields of Arcturian activations. In our consciousness, it was a crystalline Merkabah with a light igniting it. Our consciousness felt like using a springboard that traversed the dimensions and right in front of us appeared a golden walled complex. It was like a rock dressed in a golden light and as we walked towards it, the two sides went apart from the middle and there laid a grand entrance. We went inside and saw the shining corridors and how the golden lights illuminated from the stone floor.

During our first visit to the Akashic Records, we met the Guardians or the keepers of the Akashic Records. What appeared before us were three beautiful illuminated golden beings, tall with triangular-shaped heads and no facial features. They advised us to look at the corridors and the walls while setting up our intention. To our surprise, these golden corridors directed us to the area of our life where we needed to be. The memories which were stored in the area of our consciousness presented themselves as symmetrically shaped blocks that are organized into sections, just like how books in the library's shelves are. These blocks contained a moment in our life that we experienced before and it ran like a video playing in our mind.

How to release karma from your past lives with the help of the Akashic Records?

Some Records contain karmic lessons. The karma associated with a particular event is stored in the karmic field of energy that sits above the Hall of Records. Karma can be neutralized, cleared, and finally released outside your field once you acknowledge the lesson. Once karma is dissolved, this will then create a void where it once was. It is important to fill and reprogram it so the field does not invite the same negative programming again. Through communicating with your subconscious, you will be able to reboot your energetic field and program it in a way that works for your highest good. By exploring your Records, and learning the karmic lessons, you will begin to experience a profound shift in your life which will either happen straight away or a day or two afterwards. You will feel the last fragments of your emotions of your painful experiences releasing from you for the very last time. It is important that you own these emotions. Only by owning and allowing yourself to feel these, and not suppressing them, can you release it out of your energy field.

How to access your Akashic Record?

You can access your own Akashic Records as long as you can direct your consciousness to move where it needs to go. You may try connecting to high frequency beings just like we did when the Pleiadians helped us or find someone who can take your consciousness into that high vibrational state. There are no special passwords, rituals or activities needed to access your own record.

You may also seek help from other spiritually awakened people who can also help you access your Akashic Records as long as you give them the consent to enter your energy field. Our energy field is sacred and reflects our current emotional state so we must properly discern on whom we should hand out the key to our soul's library. Further, meditation is a great avenue to access your Akashic Record but that alone is not enough. Meditating will get you into the state that you need to be in, but it is more of a preparation for the journey. People often think that mediation is the finish line when it is only a tool for you to come into a point of zero of stillness.

How to read the Akashic Records?

Going through this Akashic Record is just as real as anything around us. Physical and metaphysical worlds both exist in different planes of perception. It is just that we tend to look at consciousness in a different way as not everything makes sense according to what fits in our five senses of reality. Anything that our logical mind cannot comprehend tends to be pushed aside. But in a metaphysical sense, if we can only read the aura of the people around us, we would learn that each one of us has past life memories that make up who we are in our present lifetime. If we start acknowledging these, everything will start to make sense. There will be a massive shift in our perception. We live in this 3D physical, matrix-like world where we are governed by various systems and societal constructs controlling our choices. Through accessing your Akashic Records and reprogramming your life, you will free yourself from the limiting beliefs and begin to experience a blissful living on our planet Earth. Unmasking this 3D reality will reveal what you truly are — a soul energy igniting love and light.

Information By: Aeron Lazar – Medium

Guide to the Akashic Records - Can You Really See Into Your Past, Present, Future?

What are the akashic records?

The Akashic Records are a collection of all human events, thoughts, words, emotions, and intent to have ever occurred in the past, present, and future. They're a record of each soul's journey to the infinite, and they exist on a non-physical plane. Basically, think of them as "The Book of Life" with a dash of quantum physics thrown in.

What do you mean they're not on the physical plane?

Without getting too deep into quantum physics, according to the Records, they exist in another dimension called the Akasha. Not unlike String Theory (if you're familiar), the Akashic Records is basically like a database that exists in the Akasha dimension. It's a collection of what is happening in the past, present, and future—all of the universes that are co-existing together.

What do they do?

Accessing our Akashic Records can help guide us in many ways. It can help to clear karma from our past lives and allow us to unblock areas that might unconsciously be holding us back. The biggest benefit one can get from opening the Akashic Records is getting to know oneself—why you are the way you are, why you react the ways that you do, why you are preconditioned to think certain ways. It's all in the Records.

How can you read them?

Some people can access Records by doing past life regression. It's a good way to find out more about and clear your past life trauma. Or you can locate a certified Akashic Record teacher that can help lead you through your Records. Believer, or not, it's definitely an interesting idea. And let's be honest, who wouldn't want to clear past life karma, and make way for the limitless bountiful life we all deserve?

Information By: Francesca Gariano – Necessite

Akashic Records – A Complete Guide!

When discussing Akashic records, often the visuals of a massive library comes to mind. They are thought to be the repository of all the knowledge of the universe. Some equate them to the book of life and some consider them as a mystical supercomputer.

What Are The Akashic Records?

Akashic records are as the name suggests records. But these are the universe's divine database. This heavenly library records every thought, intent, and action of every living and non-living entity in all of the worlds (parallel universes). The term 'akashic record,' comes from the Sanskrit word 'Akasha.' Akasha means the sky or space. Akashic records are considered to be present on a different plane. It is believed to be a nonphysical plane that exists at a higher level of vibrations. While the term akashic record gives the right idea of being a source of information. It gives a wrong idea to people where they believe the records to be physical books. The akashic records are not books that are found in a mystical plane. They are a stream of information that is repeatedly getting updated. They can be thought of as a divine database that is constantly updated with each new thought and actions of individuals. Similar to the existence of the records in the ethereal plane, the records are also in ethereal forms.

These records have the accounts of every human, plant, and animal that ever existed on earth. It contains accounts of what had happened in the past. It further records what is happening in the present. Again, it also records the different versions of the future. Even more interesting fact about the akashic records is that the rules of time and space don't apply here. This is because the akashic records exist in a higher plane. This fact enables the entrant of akashic records to access any information they want. This means a person can find out what had happened millions of years ago. Plus, they can get their hands on the information of any person who existed in any century. For them, accessing information of the past becomes as easy as accessing the information of the present and future.

Akashic Records – Experts Opinions

Edgar Cayce the famous psychic who is also known as the sleeping prophet popularized the akashic records. According to him, the Akashic records are not just records or memories of things that happened. Instead, he said that the akashic records influence our everyday lives. He pointed out that the records have an influence over our relationships, jobs, personality, and belief systems. Edgar also said that the records can help us understand our potential and where we are headed.

Edgar regarded the records as the universe's divine supercomputer. That recorded everything. According to him, there is an akashic record for our soul, plants, house, pets, and even our relationships. He also highlighted that akashic records connect every one of us together. In this akashic plane, we have a collective consciousness.

Linda Howe is another popular expert in the field of Akashic records. She says that the akashic records have the ability to transform our lives for the better. Accessing the knowledge of the records can help us choose the right path in life. Previously accessing the records was only limited to shamans, mystics, and great spiritual teachers. However, Linda highlights that now in the modern-day every individual has grown to become a higher soul. For this, each one of us can get a look at the records, if we want. Since the records are said to present different versions of the future, one can get a glimpse of where they are headed. If the present actions do not show a great future, an individual can correct their ways. In this sense, Akashic records can save us from devastation.

Use of Akashic Records

The akashic records can be used for different reasons. Similar to the varied interpretation of the akashic records, there are varied uses of its knowledge. The use of the records is however highly subjective to an individual's desire.

Broadly speaking, the akashic records can be accessed for the following reasons:

- Akashic records conserve and convey information. For this reason, people can rely on Akashic records to get an answer to their specific question.
- The akashic records have the potential to guide individuals on their right path. It can allow people to realize their true soul purpose. Mostly the messages through the records come via an individual's spirit guide or angel. Therefore, praying to your spirit guides during the meditative state can bring forth answers.
- In one's day to day life, it is easy to lose connection with oneself. In such cases, akashic records can be of immense help. It is believed that one's past deeds have an influence over one's present life. Since these records store everything about a soul, one can learn the reason behind their hardships.
- Going for akashic record sessions has another great benefit. It can help heal your emotional trauma. The records can help you understand why it was necessary to go through a difficult life event. When you understand why it was necessary to feel the emotional pain you can allow yourself to heal.
- The divine records have been present from the dawn of creation. Therefore, it has information about everything and everyone. For the people who want to know the hidden truths of the universe, the akashic records are a valuable treasure.
- Further, any person who wants to be in tune with himself can seek the help of the records. When the right questions are asked, the akashic records can help the person to become spiritually awakened.

History of the Akashic Records

A prominent figure of theosophy, Helena Blavatsky was one of the first people who made references to the akashic records. Upon inquiry from her disciples, Helena revealed that she gained the knowledge about the records from the Tibetan monks. The Tibetan monks considered the akashic records to be present in an ethereal plane or akasha. In eastern culture, akasha is regarded as a vital element in the '5 elements of life' philosophy. According to the eastern beliefs, all of the worlds (i.e. all the planets and galaxies) have been derived from the akasha (or space). Therefore, the akasha is a part of each organism. It has its influence over the world around us. The akashic records have existed from the beginning of time. It is the only original source of knowledge from which humans can learn. From ancient times, Indian sages, mystics, shamans, and monks have been accessing its divine knowledge. The references of the records can be found in almost all religions. It is just known with different names.

Rudolf Steiner was a well-known clairvoyant and philosopher of his time. He also referenced the akashic records. Rudolf Steiner admitted that the records exist and that every thought and action of individuals are recorded. The akashic plane is believed to be walked by spirit guides and guardian angels. Though an account of every single deed is recorded, the guardians of the records do not judge. The spirit guides access them to help their beloved humans. However, some cultures do believe that the akashic records are used to judge the fate of a soul. In today's time, more and more people are getting awakened. This has led many modern humans to discover their life's purpose through the akashic records.

How Do The Akashic Records Affect Our Lives?

When people first discover the records, their curiosity leads them to this question:

How do the records affect us?

Akashic records have a heavy influence on us and the universe. It can be thought of as the divine mind of the universe. Even though the record doesn't judge, it does play a vital role in connecting us with each other. The records connect multiple souls with each other in different lives. All the archetypal personalities and symbolism can be found in the akashic books. The records have the ability to draw individuals to each other. This means the records can make people cross paths with others. On the other hand, it also possesses the power of instilling a repelling force between individuals. This might be the reason why we are attracted to some people and repelled by some. The akashic records know about the journey of a soul. Therefore, they do play a role in bringing new people and events in someone's life. The records can push people to discover their true selves. Every human behavior and actions can be found in the records. In reality, the records have the ability to shape our conscious Masters and teachers in the past have accessed the akashic records to ascend their same can be done by people today with the knowledge of the records. People who are interested in past life regression can attempt to access the records. We are not born remembering our purpose, but accessing the records can make us remember.

The following types of individuals should definitely go for akashic record reading:

- People who want to receive information about their past life
- Who wants to take full responsibility for their present life
- Individuals who want to know about their soul's journey
- Have a yearning to return home
- People who want to heal the ailments suffered by their physical body

Who Can Read Akashic Records?

In theory, anyone can read the akashic records, if they want to. You do not have to be a mountain-dwelling sage to get access to the records. Yes, though the existence of the records has been hidden for a long time. But, truthfully its knowledge was actually incomprehensible than hidden. Now that times have changed, people are keen on raising their vibrations. They have opened up their consciousness for greater knowledge. Meaning, now more people are able to access the records and more of them are able to understand it. Sometimes the akashic records can be accessed unknowingly. In such cases, people even don't realize that they have received information from the records. You see, the akashic records exist in an ethereal plane. They are present in a sea of fluctuating energies. When the consciousness of people gets tuned in to a particular frequency they can access the records. This can even happen unintentionally. An example of this phenomenon is the random intuition people get in their daily lives. It can be as mundane as predicting a rainy day or as significant as sensing an impending accident.

Akashic Records Reading

While there are unintentional incidents, people can access the records when they want to. But this will take some practice. This can be done through regular meditation and prayer. In a meditative state, our brain opens up to new dimensions. Akashic records are also present in one such dimension. However, the most important thing while attempting to enter the akashic realms is having pure and clear intentions. There are some people who have reported to access the records in their first attempt. It is possible to do that for some. It all depends on their level of consciousness. For others, it may take some time before they can access the records. Don't lose heart in such cases.

What Happens When You Open The Akashic Records?

The internet has abundant recounts of people and their experiences with the akashic plane. If you have gone through them, you will notice that the akashic plane is different for everyone. While some recount the akashic world to be in a temple environment, some say it is more like a movie of their past lives. Some people even say that they entered the akashic realm through astral projection. Their experience was also different. For them, the akashic realm constituted of white light and divine beings. With so many different recounts, it can be well established that the akashic record will appear unique to you as well. Even though the experience is different for everyone, there is one common element to them. After entering the Akashic realm, people feel extraordinarily peaceful. The akashic plane exudes a feeling of wholeness and love. Spiritual beings can be seen walking in the realm. Some people have come forward to say that akashic records are like a gigantic library. Here the books are not written in a known language. But understanding the language is also not necessary since the books speak to you. It has been indicated in people's recollection that the books and the spirit guides speak to them telepathically.

How to Access the Akashic Records?

As mentioned before the akashic realm can be entered unintentionally. But your aim should be to get access to the records when you want to. This will allow you to derive information that helps you in some way in the present. You might not get entry to the realm in your first attempt, practicing the method will improve your chances.

The akashic records can be entered with the following steps:

1) Have clear intentions

It can't be stressed enough how important it is to have clear intentions when accessing the records. Clarity is what will help you inch closer to enter the akashic realms. Confusion and a haphazard train of thought will just hamper your chances. Take some time (a few hours or days) to arrive at a question. Be clear on why you want to get answers to it and how it can help you in your present life.

2) Be clear on what you want to ask

When you are done with your intentions, it is now time to ask the right question. Most of the time, people make the mistake of asking a vague question. This often results in no response or even unsatisfactory answers. Focus on the specifics. Think if this is the right question to ask. Further always concentrate on how the answer to it will benefit you. In the beginning, it is best to stick to one or two questions. As you become an expert, you can have a list of questions.

3) Sit in a quiet place

While accessing the records choose a quiet place to sit down. You shouldn't be disturbed or distracted at this time. To make a connection with your spirit guide or angels you can also do a prayer. Plus, you can also chant a mantra if you feel it will make you more receptive to the heavenly entities. Any time and any place are right for attempting to access the records. However, it is important that you are comfortable, receptive, and not distracted. It is best to meditate in the early morning or late at night. This will give you the quiet time that you need to make a connection.

4) Meditate on the subject of your question

You can ask whatever you want. But it is advisable if you stick to a particular topic. For example, if you are going to ask about issues with your spouse, it is best if you meditate on relationships. Again, if you want to know what is going to happen in your professional life? Meditate on how you have landed a particular position and how your work is going.

5) Introduce yourself to anyone you encounter

The akashic realms are unchartered territory for you. You don't know who you will encounter. The realm is said to be walked by spirit guides, angels, and other souls like you. Whoever you meet it is essential that you introduce yourself and state your intentions. You never know, if that entity may just have been waiting to guide you. Again, if you encounter souls like you, who are looking for answers, introduce yourself. Chances are they are or may have been connected with you.

6) Ask your question aloud

After beginning the process of accessing the akashic records, for a few minutes, meditate. When you feel that you are slipping into a receptive state start focusing on your question. Ponder on it some more. Lastly, think about why you want that question answered and ask that question out loud.

Your question can be anything like:

I have been working for 3 years in the XYZ Company as a team leader. Where is my professional life headed?

7) Wait for a response

After you have asked your question aloud, it's time for the universe to give you an answer. Therefore, be patient and wait. The answer may not come immediately so you can keep focusing on the question till then.

If even after waiting for 10 to 15 minutes you don't get an answer then end the session. Many people can't access the akashic record in the beginning. But after multiple attempts, they did get success. You just need to repeat this mindful session a few times more. There are also some Akashic guided meditations that can help you in this endeavor.

8) Try to interpret the received answer

When you receive an answer from the akashic records, it may not be so clear. You may need to figure out what the answer means. Also, the messages may come in different forms. The message can be a visual or auditory message. It can also come in the form of taste, sensation, or even smell. So be aware of your senses.

9) Keep repeating the above steps

Even if you are able to access the record in the first attempt, it will take some time to make sense of the answers. Therefore, you need to keep repeating these steps to get better at interpreting the messages.

10) Write down your experience

Sometimes the answer may not make sense to you when you are in the session. Therefore, it is advisable to write down what you saw or heard. Recount what was your experience and write it down in detail. Forget about it for a day. The next day read what you have written. This will give you a fresh perspective on your experience. Things that were not apparent before may become clear later.

Akashic Field: A Place beyond Time and Space

In the earlier sections, it has been already mentioned that the akashic field is beyond time and space. In this dimension of the universe, the rules of time and space do not apply. What is often represented as a plane or even dimension is sometimes referred to as a field. A field that was present from the beginning of time itself. This field is called the Akashic field. The akashic field predates time. Ancient scholars believed that this field is the originator of our world. This means our world has emerged from the akashic field. In a 2014 interview, Mr. Deepak Chopra revealed that cosmologists believe the universe is constantly created from the Akashic field. It happens from a phenomenon called eternal inflation. Cosmologists believe that this subtle sea of fluctuating field is responsible for the creation and sustenance of our world. The concepts of the akashic field will become clear to you if you compare it with the quantum mechanics of physics. According to sciencemag.org, physicists have done an experiment to know more about the nature of the photon. With the experiments done on space, it has been found that photons can behave both as a matter and a wave. It appears in these two different forms depending on how they tried to measure it. From this experiment, it was concluded that reality too depends on how we perceive it. It is up to the people to choose how they see reality. From these data and experiments, the universe and its origins seem so mysterious. What physics now shows through quantum mechanics had already been mentioned in ancient cultures.

Ervin Laszlo on Akashic Field Theory

Ervin Laszlo is a science philosopher. He is a Hungarian pianist who is also a visiting faculty at the Graduate Institute Bethany. Ervin Laszlo is one of the founders of a secret group called General Evolutionary Research. The primary aim of this group was to learn about the evolution of the world and humanity. Ervin Laszlo is one of those esteemed professors who believe that the knowledge of science and religion are not exclusive of each other. He is also a supporter of the Akashic field theory. In 2004, Laszlo published a book named 'Science and the Akashic Field: An Integral Theory of Everything.' In this book, Laszlo pointed out that the universe emerges from the Akashic field. Further, he states that the Akashic field consists of the universe's information. In his book, Laszlo proposes that this field is the quantum vacuum (or point akashic field) from which information is conveyed to the universe. This is an intelligent field that carries the memory of the universe. This intelligent field is responsible for the creation and running of the atoms and galaxies. The teachings of Ervin Laszlo also suggest that evolution and creation of complex organisms is not a chance occurrence. This intelligent field or the point akashic field has an integral role in giving it the present form.

Visiting the Akashic Records and Akashic Memory

The Akashic Memory holds information about our experiences and what we have seen from past lives or can experience within the akashic record. An example of an akashic records experience could be looking at Atlantean healing grids and what the Atlantean languages looked like with healing symbols.

Seeing how the WingMakers language is based on a similar dialect to the Atlantean languages. The WingMakers are an advanced civilization of galactic humanoids who come from the future and left time capsules for humans to find on Earth with wisdom based technology for our soul and physical evolution to be advanced through their higher dimensional teachings. There are chambers with artwork and disc technology in the Arrow project.

Meeting aspects of one's past life selves like the Atlantean Dragon protectors that are female who are named Raylana and Kelala as well as one of the mermaid aspects named Jalina who wrote in the Atlantean healing languages. The aspects of the past life selves showed how they had worked with creating healing murals in Atlantean languages so those murals could be turned into healing grids. Being in the akashic records had cleared feeling tired, fatigued, and added a boost in rejuvenation of fresh energy to no longer feel sick.

While visiting the akashic records there was a familiar being that was seen. Her name is Marisha she is a records wisdom keeper and a soul reader who sees the divine balance of soul paths in human lives, she travels among the stars collecting higher knowledge wisdom information to help guide living beings in physical bodies on their ascension paths, as well she is the sage of the wise wisdom in the ages when turning the akashic records pages. Marisha is energetically part of the sea in life creation as she creates the living light of the universe to help expand its growth cycles and to oscillate it at higher vibrational frequencies so it too evolves to resonate at increasing octaves while it upgrades itself.

Final Thoughts

There are several mysteries hidden beneath the fabric of reality. Though the knowledge of the Akashic records has been present since ancient times, it is only now that we comprehend it. The Akashic records hold divine information that can make people's lives better. Tuning our consciousness to the Akashic field can uncover the truth of our existence.

Information By: Sujata Deb – Soul Mind Connection, Ileana Ka

The Akashic Records

The Holographic Archives of the Universe

A great deal of information is available from the akashic records. Those familiar with the akashic records tend to think of them as a place, like the reference library of the cosmos. However, the akashic records are everywhere, part of the fabric of all things. Everything that occurs is recorded there. Anyone can learn to access this information, at least to some degree. However, the records are quite complex and require a great deal of practice to use skillfully.

What Are the Akashic Records?

The core of the akashic records is the akashic plane, the neutral plane. It is the overall record for the universe. The akashic plane interpenetrates the other six planes through their "local" akashic records. For example, our physical body has an akashic record of all that it has experienced; that record will ultimately be distilled and integrated into the akashic plane.

Since the akashic plane is adjacent to the causal and mental planes, essences focused on those planes can access it most easily. Some psychics directly access at least the surface of the akashic plane. However, from the physical plane, it is not possible to go very deeply into it. Accessing the akashic plane is not really what your lessons are about on the physical plane, and you are not designed for it. This is one reason you find it useful to channel sources such as ourselves. It is germane to our lessons to delve into the akashic plane. We are learning to do this, and we can access information that might be inaccessible to you. We are not discouraging you from trying to access it yourselves, but we can help in this way. Although psychics may have limited access to the akashic plane, they can have full access to the physical plane akashic records, which are not yet fully distilled. The instinctive (neutral) center is the location of a person's individual akashic records; it interpenetrates the other centers and stores their memories there; it is the seat of the subconscious. The individual instinctive center is, in turn, connected to larger "storehouses," such as the collective consciousness of humanity. Ultimately, it is connected to the whole, so when we clarify our instinctive center through self-knowledge and healing, we are contributing to the clarification of the whole physical universe. Also, as our essence integrates the reincarnational self we are in this lifetime, our akashic records become more accessible to our whole essence, and ultimately, our records will be distilled into the akashic plane, contributing to the knowledge of all the planes and the Tao. Scholars, being the neutral role, play a special part in this distillation process. So the integration simultaneously moves outward, from the individual to the whole physical plane, and upward, through the astral and causal planes to the akashic plane.

The instinctive center, and the akashic records in general, store memories in whatever way they were experienced and understood, irrespective of any "ultimate truth." If the information is organized and clear, it is because the experience it records was clear, or was later clarified; the information doesn't necessarily naturally occur that way. For instance, some types of information, such as traumatic past lives, may be difficult to get clearly if the original confusion around them is still there. On the other hand, Michael Reading chart information, which is based on an akashic records reading, is usually clear because it consists of specific choices made by a person's essence. There is no distillation of the akashic records except through the evolution of those who had the experiences those records record. If you had a traumatic experience in the past and you dealt with it—if you evolved your experience of that trauma—that, too, goes into the records. What ultimately remains on the akashic plane is the distillation, what was learned, which is what is relevant for the universe to carry forward into the future. The rest is compost, breaking down into its component parts. This distillation is constantly occurring as you continue to grow. It happens within you as a personality, and within your essence, entity, cadre, and so forth. When you pick up unfinished pieces from the past and see them with more clarity and understanding, you evolve the experience. The akashic records appear to you as a literal record of things exactly as they occurred that can be replayed and looked at from different angles: each person experiences an event differently, and all those experiences are recorded. Everything that ever was is recorded, including the smallest minutiae—the falling of a tree in a forest is recorded. However, it is not that a very extensive supply of VHS tape running through all reality is constantly being imprinted. The real explanation lies in the nature of time itself: the akashic records are actually windows into the past; they go into the neutral space directly above the time-space continuum and allow one to look into another time without actually going into that time—it is strictly a window, a place from which to view. Since there is an infinitely long past, this could be overwhelming, but what you end up attracting to your vision is what has some relevance to you, some reason for you to see. Your being on a particular piece of land, for instance, automatically biases your looking into the akashic records to the records of that land, unless you specifically ask for something else. And why would someone see a particular event that occurred on that land, and not one of a million others back to the time it was ocean or even gas? A particular story is attracted in your presence because of something in it that resonates with you.

In Yarbro, Michael refers to the akashic plane as a "photographic record." In fact, all akashic records could be thought of as photographic, or perhaps holographic aspect, since they are not merely visual, but multidimensional—when we look through the "window" the records provide, we see the total experience. We could think of it as being in a "code" similar to the digital information that is found on compact discs and CD-ROMs (which are all zeros and ones), rather than in language as we know it. Therefore, as with photographs or videos, when the code of a particular event is accessed and "played back," there are many ways it can be translated into language and interpreted. Also, there is far more in the code than is readily communicated in language, so it is wise not to take any translation of the akashic records as the final word.

Different channeled entities sometimes give conflicting, or at least apparently conflicting, versions of everything from how the universe operates and the history of the Earth, to what we are meant to eat. To illustrate why, let's look at one example: a hypothetical car accident. As is well known, if you ask twenty bystanders what happened, you are likely to get twenty at least slightly differing accounts, as well as those from the people who were in the accident. Journalists are supposedly trained to be objective, and if one is present, you would expect that he could tell you what really happened, but different journalists can also give conflicting accounts. However, you can probably piece together a good idea of what happened if you compare enough accounts and see where the common threads are. Let's say that fifty years later, a nonphysical entity is researching that accident in order to answer a question about it at a channeling session. The "pictures" of everyone's subjective experience of that accident are in the akashic records. Whose account will the entity rely on? It might be useful for the entity to consult several. Even if many of those accounts show pictures of the accident itself with reasonable objectivity, these are also subject to interpretation, and may not completely show the factors that led to the accident.

The Los Angeles Rodney King beating was on videotape, but a jury in the first trial still found the police officers innocent—they interpreted the pictures differently than most people did (which led to riots). What is the ultimate truth about the beating? Were the officers justified under the circumstances? We have to decide for ourselves, and to do so fairly would require a good deal of research and mature judgment. Our court system is supposed to provide this kind of research and mature judgment, but we all know that it often fails to do this. Similarly, nonphysical entities must research and exercise wise judgment, based on deep understanding, in order to accurately interpret akashic records. They need to come from a neutral space holding no bias towards anything and only showing the facts of the true information contained in the akashic records as it had really happened in the events that transpired in space and in the cosmos. There is no absolute version of reality and no ultimate source of information that can rightly say, "No, this is how it really happened—guaranteed." Everything in the akashic records was recorded by a consciousness with a particular point of view, and the records are vast. That's why it's worthwhile to explore a variety of points of view. It is true that the Tao as a whole is the ultimate source for the universe, but it is concerned with the large picture, just as the CEO of a major corporation would not be the one to tell you exactly what went on in a sales meeting in the field somewhere.

Channeled entities are in a process of growth and evolution, just as we are. And just as reading books and working with teachers and groups may assist our growth, it is similar for them. They have their teachers, groups, and "books," only their books are nonphysical—they are in the akashic records. And channeled entities, like us, are not all reading the same books. The information they give us depends on what they've been reading. Everything in the records was someone's experience of what happened; therefore, none of it can be said to be "wrong." A challenge for a channeled entity is to interpret the records from the highest and most inclusive point of view. The highest truth is the synthesis of all elements of truth in every point of view. The akashic records, then, do not provide instant knowledge. Information must be gathered and interpreted; this is an art as well as a science.

Information By: **Shepherd Hoodwin – Michaelteachings**

Seeing Pyramids, Portals, and Time Line Traveling in the Akashic Records

When viewing someone's Akashic Records there can be various examples of their lifetimes of past lives and various historical events that can be seen in their records like building pyramids in Atlantis and Egypt, building portals on Earth with white light magic to create stable ley lines, doing time line traveling and creating a new universe where sentient lifeforms exist as well as learning about Atantean and Lemurian transformational languages that create positive manifestation in people's lives. As well as seeing a beings Akashic Book of Life.

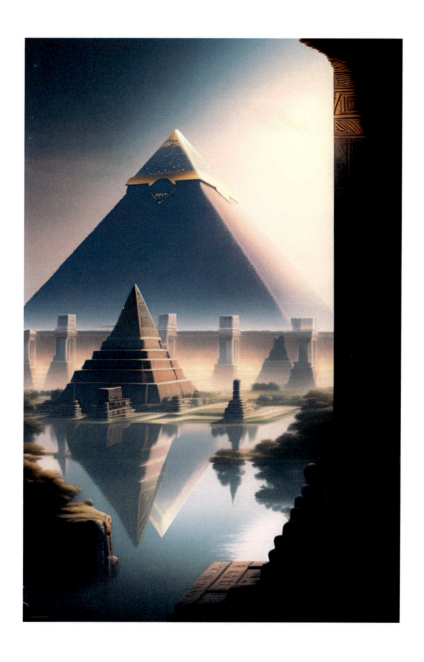

Building pyramids in Atlantis and Egypt.

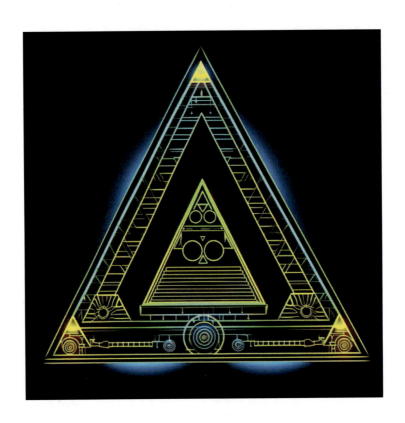

Light circuitry pyramid.

Pyramid codes.

Lay line portal codes.

Time line portal jumping and changing time line history.

Time travel portal gateways on ancient Earth.

Creating the cosmic web so that space portals
can be formed as time dilation bridge paths
to make new universes in the multiverse.

Creating a new universe sphere that exists within the bigger multiverse sphere. Universes have sentient consciousness and upgrade themselves energetically to higher oscillation frequencies and energetic fields. There are younger universes and also older types of universes, some of the universes are experimental places where various lifeforms and soul consciousness's are created as part of living library repositories for expanded life creation systems.

Crystalline pyramids built in Atlantis.

Portal gateway pyramids built in Atlantis.

Portal gateway pyramids built in Atlantis.

Portal gateway pyramids built in Lemuria.

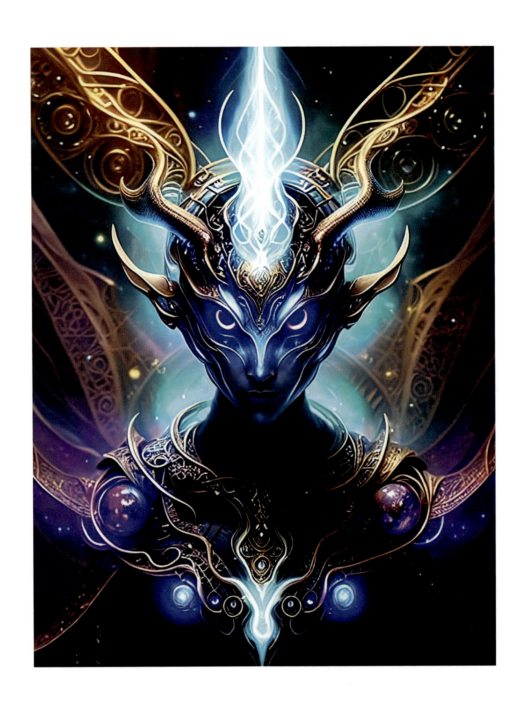

Jasa a higher self aspect in the Akashic Records.

Jasa a higher self aspect in the Akashic Records.

Namari a higher self aspect in the Akashic Records.

Creating magic portal gateways to other worlds.

Akashic Book of Life.

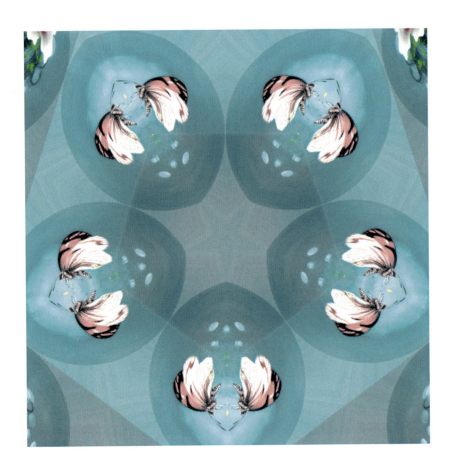

Entering the Akashic Records of a soul being.

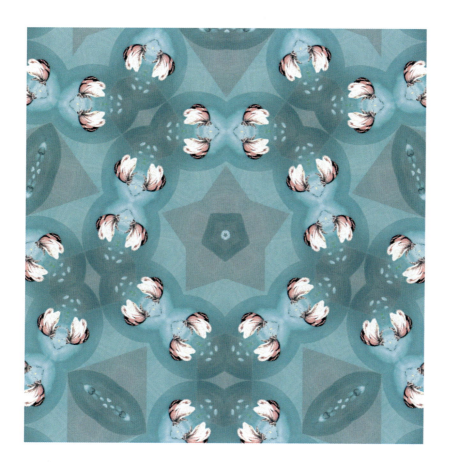

Life is always changing, and we are always evolving. The moth spirit animal can remind us to embrace change and to be open to new experiences. The moth is also a symbol of death and rebirth. In many cultures, the moth is a creature that lives in the darkness and only comes out at night.

The symbol of the moth also signifies a time of transformation and learning about yourself to discover who you truly are as a soul being.

Light Language in Healing Grids

Several of the healing grids in the book have light language encoded in the Atlantean and the Sirian healing vibrational frequencies within the grids that is transmitted through the light languages that are included within the sacred geometry woven within the grids.

What is Light Language?

Light Language is an umbrella term used to describe various languages of other dimensional Beings such as the Galactic Light Beings, as well as languages of forgotten civilizations that existed here on Earth such as Lemuria and Atlantis. Light Language can also designate the unique sound of your Soul. But most importantly, Light Language is a potent spiritual tool that has long been misunderstood and underused due to lack of insight.

In this written communication you will learn the following:

- What is Light Language?
- How to "learn" Light Language?
- What is a Light Language activation and what is Light Language transmission?
- How can you tell if it is genuine Light Language and not gibberish?
- Can you understand Light Language?
- Benefits and practical applications of speaking Light Language

Many people who can channel mystical sounds that resemble a language are perplexed as they don't know where it comes from, what it means and how to use it.

When someone first activates the ability to speak or write in Light Language they may not have any clue what they have channeled, where it originated or how powerful it was! Currently, many sacred geometry practitioners speak multiple different light languages, including Arcturian, Pleiadian, Sirian, Lyran, Avian and Lyran Feline, Lemurian, Atlantean, Mintaka, Blue Avian (Azurites) and the Language of the Akashic Keepers. More importantly, we can distinguish between them, understand them and activate the ability to channel Language of Light in other people. Our goal is to bring more conscious understanding to the subject of Light Language so more people can use it intentionally for transformation, connection and healing. But first thing first...

Everything in thought consciousness and creation is connected by the quantum energetics of sound vibration, frequency coded sequencing of energy and physical manifestation that embodies itself in the holographic field of the universe and then also in solid matter in the various universes that exist within the vastness of the harmonic multiverse. Light Language, sacred geometry, crystalline essence, the field of the Akasha in unified quantum fields of collective experiences and know along with the Akashic Records are all here. The Akashic Records can feel like an individualized experience in seeing sacred symbols, a book of life, energetic frequency of awareness in seeing events unfold from the past, present or the future, this can all be experienced in varied sensations, nothing will look or feel the same to every individual when they are accessing their Akashic Records. Some aspects of learned knowledge and experience of all living beings and creators goes within the collective unified field where everyone can access knowledge of how things work, understanding experiencing knowing guidance, etc. These collective guidance's of information do not contain who contributed it to the unified field, there are no names or events mentioned just the collective information we can tap into to learn and grow from valuable experiences and knowledge to help us evolve and ascend.

There are planetary, galactic, universe, and individual Akashic Records within the Akasha that people can tap into. Some can quickly find what they need to see within their Akashic Records in terms of information about past lives by energetically scrolling through events, history, and experiences of what they have done or lived through within their Akashics others will need to work with their guides or guardians to access specific information within their Akashic Records. Each individuals Akashic Records are guarded and protected by energetic frequency seals that have protective symbols on them and those seals are specifically coded for those beings to enter into their Akashic Records. There could be Akashic Record Keepers that may work within sophisticated records to guide you on your journey of exploring the Akashic Records and to open portions of your records to find information about your soul mission, purpose in life, who you are, what galactic lifetimes you have lived, Earth lifetimes, if you have embodied Angelic beings, etc. As well there are degrees of Akaschic Records readers some can access the surface of your soul field Akashic Records of who you have been and what you have done while others can go into the core of your deepest aspects of the Akashic Records to see every piece of information and knowledge that resides within your Akashic Records. The Akashic Records are like vast knowledge library repositories of information and experiences of everything that exists within creation itself so there are protocols for respecting the different environments within Akashic Records that are accessed by having permission to go through the seals of someone Akashic Records and explore their history, if permission is not given to access your own records or someone else's then likely there is some important reason for that which might have to do with your safety, protection, information could be classified or someone could need more time to become accustomed to the Akashic Records in immersing themselves in how they connect with the Akasha.

What is Light Language?

Light Language is not really one language. This is one of the biggest misconceptions. Light Language is actually an umbrella term that encompasses various languages of so-called Galactic Light Beings such as the Arcturians, the Pleiadians, the Sirians, the Lyrans, and the Andromedans. Light Language can also mean languages of forgotten civilizations that existed here on Earth such as Lemuria and Atlantis. And last but not least, people also refer to Light Language when they mean to describe the unique sound of their Soul.

Our favorite definition of Light Language is channeling energy in the form of sound. And you can channel any energy in that way: the energy of Galactic Beings, the energy of land and the essence of your Soul. In that way, Light Language is not necessarily just a form of verbal communication — it is also a transfer of energy.

Light Language can be a memory of Language that your Soul has spoken in your previous incarnations. But most importantly, Light Language is a potent spiritual modality similar to other forms of sound and energy healing. It can be used to raise your vibration, rid the atmosphere of any negative energies and even to heal.

How can I learn Light Language?

The bad news is that you cannot learn Light Language! But the good news is that you don't have to. Light Language is an ability that already lies dormant within you, waiting to be activated.

Light Languages can come from three different sources: either from the memory of Languages you spoke in one of your past lifetimes (be it here on Earth or elsewhere in the Galaxy), straight from your soul or from some external energy, such as the energy of the land.

As such, there are three ways of activating Light Language

Extraterrestrial Light Languages such as Arcturian or Sirian or Pleiadian or languages from Earth's ancient civilizations of Lemuria and Atlantis get activated when you come into contact with strong spiritual energies of Light Beings and intend to activate them. Then as memories of your previous incarnations awaken, you just need to open your mouth and the language will flow.

Whenever these languages are activated (it can be experienced about 15 times with various languages), you can literally feel an incoming download of information, and then your mouth would open here it is: a new language.

But there is also a second way of activating a Light Language: it's awakening the Language of your Soul. When we discovered the Language of our Higher Self, it came from within. It's got a unique sound. It's different and unlike any of the other languages. It comes with melody and it represents our very essence.

The Soul Language does not need activating or downloading: it is always there. The "only" thing you need to do is to strip all the layers, densities, karma, trauma, perceptions, stories… It is not a clean, quick, beautiful or exciting experience: it can take diligence and dedication and letting go of karmic, past-life and this life and ancestral programmes. The reward is well worth it though and goes beyond just activating the Language of your Soul. You will feel lighter and happier than ever before.

Finally, to channel external energies in the form of Light Language such as the elemental beings or spirit of the land, you just need to connect to it and let it flow. We discovered this actually quite accidentally. First time, when we were meditating in Broome, Western Australia, we had sat on ancient rocks, marked by dinosaur's footprints. We had connected to the Spirit of the Land and tapped into the Song Line. The Language that came out was very similar to the language we often heard on a local Aboriginal Radio Station. The second time it happened when we were coming to land over the Yucatan Peninsula in Mexico and started channeling the language on the aircraft.

What is a Light Language transmission or a Light Language activation?

Light Language Activation can mean one of two things: either activation of your ability to speak Light Language in you or using Light Language to heal or activate certain aspects of your life. When you combine the power of intention with the frequencies of Light Language, true magic happens. In a Light Language transmission, a person uses Light Languages as a tool for reprogramming your energetic field for a specific purpose.

It can be a flow of love, abundance, vitality, healing, creativity, manifestation — you name it. During transmission Light Language is used as a coding device for energy to work deep beyond the levels of conscious or even subconscious mind and to repair or rewire energetic patterns that may be negatively affecting your day to day life.

How do Light Languages compare to regular human languages?

Each Light Language has a unique sound and energy signature. Some Light Languages can sound like regular languages, some sound nothing like human language. But the most important distinction between a normal language and light language is the energy and frequency contained in the languages of light.

For example, the Language of the Akashic Keepers sounds like chants and comes with melody and tonality. Blue Avian (Azurites) Language sounds like bird chirps.

But there are Light Languages that sound very similar to earthly languages. For example, Lemurian Light Language sounds very similar to languages of the Pacific Islands — not surprisingly. We remember a few days after our Lemurian activated, we had walked into a local shop and overheard a dialogue between two women who looked like they were of Pacific descent. The similarities nearly brought us to tears.

As for other Languages — Arcturian sounds very Middle-Eastern, a bit like Arabic or Hebrew. But as someone who learnt the basics of Hebrew and Arabic — we know it's just common sounds, but the actual words are totally different.

Lyran Languages, especially Lyran Feline, remind us of Spanish. Reptilian sounds a bit like Vietnamese. We are trying to describe it as best as we can but it may be easier if you actually listen to some samples of someone speaking several of those languages. Light languages can be accessed to be performed in channeling various Light Languages in recorded videos. All Light Languages have a unique frequency that taps into a person's soul field and it can reveal information about someone's Starseed Origins, galactic lifetimes, vibrational ability to heal with sound frequency, etc. hence practitioners who are adapt at these abilities are sometimes called Light Language Readers.

How do you tell between Light Language and "gibberish"?

As someone who activates Light Language ability in other people and receives multiple audio samples from different individuals daily we can tell you, we have never heard "gibberish". Every single Light Language sample we have received was real. But it is important to note that not every so-called Light Language is of the Light — some actually belong to negative alien Races such as the Reptilians or the Draconians. But the most important thing is the energy in the transmission — Light Languages carry potent frequencies, able to activate and transform your day to day life. One time someone had been suggesting that "anyone can speak some mumble-jumble" for 60 seconds. We suppose anything is possible but it would take a tremendous amount of effort to keep coming up with unique sounds for a longer period of time. As a response to this, we decide to speak various languages for 20-30 minutes straight with no interruptions or background music during videos. The languages come in separate transmissions of Arcturian, Lemurian, Pleiadian, Sirian and Lyran.

Can you understand Light Language?

Now we have established that Light Language is not some made up gibberish, let's address another issue: can you actually understand what is being said. The answer is a resounding yes. Just the fact that most people don't understand as Light Language sounds foreign to them, it does not mean that you cannot get the meaning behind the words. Light Language is a transfer of both information and energy. And as such it often tells a story. We understand what we channel and we usually translate what we say right after or even during our transmissions as we don't like keeping the audience in the dark. During our Light Language Course, we train our students in decoding the meaning of Light Languages too. We witnessed time and time the simultaneous consensus in the group and how accurate and detailed their translations are. Currently, understanding Light Language has more to do with deciphering its energetic signature than with translating it word for word. However, as our collective understanding of this powerful modality deepens, understanding word for word will become more and more common. We have already experienced glimpses of word for word understanding when working with our students.

What are the benefits of speaking and listening to Light Language?

"What is the point of speaking Light Language?" was a question we had asked ourselves over the years until we discovered just how powerful and practical this modality is.

You can use the Light Language for a number of purposes:

1. You can use Light Language to discover your Soul's history including your Starseed / Earthseed origins. From our experience activating Light Languages in our students, the Language that activates first is usually the language that your Soul spoke in your last Galactic lifetime before you incarnated here on Earth as who you are today. This is why Light Language can be the answer to a question many lightworkers ask which is "What are my Starseed origins?" If you activate Artcturian — then you will know that you came here on a mission from Arcturus, if you activate Sirian — you know that your last Galactic lifetime was in the Sirius system, and so on.

2. You can use Light Language to connect to your Soul Family as Spirit Guides. As mentioned, every Light Language has its own unique energy signature. So when you speak a specific Light Language, your entire body and energy field attunes to this particular frequency. This makes connection with your Galactic Support Team much easier to establish.

3. You can use Light Language to raise your vibration and cleanse the atmosphere around you. Light Languages contain powerful positive frequencies. You can use them in the same way as a smudge stick or a Tibetan singing bowl. One of the highest vibrational Light Languages is the Pleiadian Light Language. If you want to elevate your mood, have a listen to a Pleiadian Light Language transmission. We bet you will feel energized afterwards. Someone who had listened to such a transmission claims it has healed her hangover in an instance!

4. You can use Light language to transfer Consciousness Technology that goes beyond "mindset" and works deep in a person's energy field. As already mentioned, you can use Light Language to re-code your field for optimum flow of energy. You can also partner up with Beings of Light such as the Arcturians, the Sirians or the Pleiadians to transfer powerful codes from their collective consciousness to help in every aspect of your life.

What's the purpose of Light Language?

10 practical and surprising applications of the mystical modality from the Light Language Polyglot

What's the point in speaking Light Language? That was a question we had asked ourselves for over a decade, ever since our first Light Language activated when we were in our early twenties. It felt like a party trick — quirky, otherworldly but utterly useless in our day-to-day life.

Fast forward 15 years and 20 more Light Languages have activated in ourselves and hundreds more in our students, this ability is the most important tool in our energetic toolbox.

It is still quirky and otherworldly, but utterly transformative, practical and powerful.

What's the purpose of Light Language?

Light Language is a powerful, and often underestimated energetic tool for healing, expansion and transformation. Here is a list of practical ways you can use Light Language not only in your spiritual life but in your day-to-day!

#1 To bring back ancient knowledge and memories

The common feedback we get after our transmissions — especially when people hear us channel for the very first time is that something stirred within them. A sense of familiarity and nostalgia. Flashbacks of past lives, often on other planets. A remembrance of who they really are as multidimensional beings. When they connect to this feeling they often get a sense of purpose and start seeing their life in a new light, with a fresh sense of purpose. It is often a very emotional and profound moment, when centuries-old memories stored in their energetic bodies start to flood their system.

#2 To activate spiritual gifts and abilities in other Starseeds & Lightworkers

The frequency we hold and express in Language of Light brings hidden abilities and supernatural powers to the surface, especially in Starseeds. These can be psychic, healing, channeling or activating skills that they often did not know about. They sometimes come online right after the transmission but often unfold in the days and weeks after. Light Language acts as a bridge for frequency to connect people with the abilities they have mastered in their previous incarnations.

#3 To transmit consciousness technology energetic upgrades

Consciousness Technology, often referred to as Light Codes or DNA Light Codes, are powerful energetic upgrades coming from various Galactic Races or from the fabric of the Quantum Multiverse that can rewire energetic fields beyond the conscious and subconscious mind. These upgrades result in concrete shifts in physical reality of the person receiving them and work just like magic on the energetic scales. Once you discover these advanced Quantum energetic tools, you will realize that the law of attraction that humanity has been raving on for the last decade is just the tip of the energetic iceberg. These gentle but sophisticated codes can be transmitted in Light Languages with specific area of your life in mind. They can help you to find the sense of purpose, attract more synchronicities, manifest the life of your dreams and shift into the highest state of flow, abundance, health and happiness!

#4 To communicate with Galactic Beings

Various Races of Beings of Light communicate telepathically but if you are struggling with receiving messages in a conscious or a trans-dimensional state, Light Language provides a concrete, easy alternative. You speak — and then you translate what you just said. That's right, contrary to a popular belief, you can absolutely understand what you're channeling. We often translate our Light Language transmissions in real time, and teach it to our students.

#5 To raise vibration

This is one of the most basic but very effective applications of Light Language. When you channel Light Language, your vibration naturally increases — and so does that of your clients! It is super useful whenever you are under the weight of an illness, negative energy and need to snap out of it! In our many years' experience of channeling Light Language we have even discovered that speaking Light Language helps us fend off infections — whenever our body is fighting against a flu or cold, we start channeling and the symptoms usually subside within a few hours and never come back.

#6 To discover Starseed / Earthseed origins

An activated Light Language serves as a hard proof of your Starseed or Earthseed origins. Usually the one that activates first is from your last Galactic lifetimes. So if your Arcturian activates — then you must have had an incarnation as an Arcturian. If your Pleiadian activates — then your Soul has once been a Pleiadian, and so on and so forth. Of course, as our Soul experiences different terrestrial and extraterrestrial incarnations, you may have more than one available — and both myself and our students are living proof of that!

#7 To cleanse the atmosphere

Due to its high frequency, Light Language has the ability to blast through any energetic densities — especially languages such as Blue Avian (Azurites), Orion and Pleiadian. You can use them as your own portable, weightless and discrete smudging stick or Tibetan singing bowl!

#8 To heal the physical body

Light Language is often used by healers to restore the physical body — of both humans and animals — to its optimum state of vitality. The sound frequencies work on a deep cellular level to bring about healing and transformation. This is not our particular area of specialism, but we have witnessed our students add Light Language to their healing practices with incredible results.

#9 To build Quantum Architecture

You can use Light Language to install various pieces of invisible but powerful Quantum Architecture in your own field and that of your clients — be it protective shielding, amplified business resonance, programming transformative frequency in your programmes and offering — you can use Light Language for all of that.

#10 To unblock your expression

Apart from channeling languages of various Galactic Races or ancient civilizations such as Lemuria or Atlantis, you can also activate the Language of your Soul. This unique sound expresses the very essence of who you are beyond this physical body. It is a very profound experience and one that melts various blocks to expression that often sit around our throat energy center.

The list above is not exhaustive! As we are growing in understanding of the Light Language on both collective and individual level, our understanding of this mystical modality will grow to include more precision and conscious understanding.

How Light Language can help you discover your Stareed Origins

Not many people know that Light Language — or channeling energy in the form of sound — is directly related to Starseed origins. That's because Light Language is still considered quite a strange, mystical modality and largely misunderstood.

But whilst many freshly awakened Starseeds are wasting their time reading generic and often very inaccurate lists of Starseed traits, Light Language provides a solid energetic pathway to discover which Star system you came from — and to connect with your Star Family. Let us explain how.

What is Light Language?

To begin with, you need to understand what Light Language is. The phrase "Light Language" is unfortunate and even misleading because it does not refer to a single language. One of the most common misconceptions is thinking of Light Language as one language.

But in fact, Individuals who express the distinct tone of their Soul, as well as those who channel various energies, such as energies of the land they stood on, or energies of Galactic Light Beings such as the Arcturians, Pleiadians, Sirians, Lyrans, and Andromedans, use the same term. Languages of long-forgotten civilizations such as Lemuria and Atlantis can also be referred to as Light Language. One thing they all have in common is that Light Language expresses energy through sound and harmonic frequency of tones, tunes, music, as well as acoustical expression of creative exploration in imagination of your soul essence in who you are within yourself.

So how does the Light Language relate to your Starseed origins?

Every Galactic and Inner Earth Race have their unique energetic signature. And this energy signature is expressed very strongly in their Light Language! For example, Sirian Language is grounding, Arcturian is infused with unconditional love, Lyran and Avian is sublime and carries the frequency of freedom, Lemurian is coded with divine feminine love and Atlantean — with divine masculine confidence.

However, what's more important is that the Light Language energy works beyond your conscious mind and directly into your energy field. It can awaken your dormant Soul memories.

When you hear Light Language that belongs to the Star Race that your Soul was once a member of — you will instantaneously recognize it. It will sound like an old, familiar song. You may even be strongly moved by the energy to the point of tears as your subconscious Soul memories flood your system. You may feel strong sensations in your body or just a very subtle sense of nostalgia. This is a sure fire indication that you have once spoken this Light Language and that your Soul remembers.

We remember personally when we first heard someone speaking Sirian Light Language in a guided meditation. We were already experienced in Light Languages, with over a decade of channeling Arcturian but it was the first time in this lifetime that we heard Sirian. We were in a meditative state but when the Language came through it felt like a jolt of energy and we suddenly felt like we came home! It was incredible. A few weeks later, we connected to the Sirians directly and our own Sirian activated. We accessed memories of our lifetime on Sirius as a researcher. Pieces of the puzzle fell into place.

Which leads us to another point:

Activating your own Light Language as a way of telling your Starseed roots

When your own Light Language activates, this will be a very strong, unmistakable indicator of your Starseed heritage! If you start speaking Arcturian — it means you once were an Arcturian, if you speak Pleiadian — then it means you've had an experience as a Pleiadian, and so on. Bottom-line is: Light Language taps into your Soul memories, and what determines the Light Language that will activate, is what you have experienced as a Soul. It is very rare to be able to speak a Light Language that does not come from your own Soul memories. From our experience activating light languages of hundreds of Starseeds, Light Language that activates the first is usually the one from your last Galactic incarnation before this one on Earth. And your last Galactic incarnation determines your Soul mission. After all, this has been where you answered the call to incarnate on Earth as a volunteer to help raise the collective consciousness up with the help of your Galactic superpowers. It is possible to activate more than one Light Language simultaneously. In fact, what we have noticed during our Light

Language Activations, is that as our collective understanding of Light Language deepens, more and more people activate multiple languages straight away. When we first started activating Light Languages in other Starseeds a couple of years ago, it was exceptional when a person activated more than one Light Language. Now, it is becoming a new normal feature of our energetic transmissions. This leads to another point!

As a Starseed you may have incarnated as more than one Star Being!

That's right! As a soul we often go through hundreds or even thousands of lifetimes — both here on Earth and as extraterrestrial beings. This is why labels such as "Arcturian", "Pleiadian", "Blue Avian" aka Azurites do not fully encompass our Souls' vast experiences as we could have been all three at some point! And as such you may be able to activate all three Light Languages. We currently speak 20 different ones, but that's because of our unique Soul blueprint. Our first experience as a Soul was as an Akashic Records keeper — a Galactic librarian of sorts. Having lived in the Library of the Universe as our first experience.

There is also one more important point to make:

Your Soul's origins vs your Starseed origin

Your Soul's origins — or your very first experience after separating from Source — is also something that carries like an imprint throughout your lifetimes. That imprint is also expressed in your Light Language. So to sum it up: Soul origin is determined by your Soul's very first experience, your Starseed origin — by the last experience before this earthly incarnation. What we have noticed over the course of listening to many audio samples of our students that the first Soul experience leaves an energetic trace. For example, our husband Aeron Lazar speaks Arcturian (this was his last Galactic lifetime), but you can still feel a Dragon energy imprint around him. This is because his first soul experience was as a Dragon. The same imprint is reflected in his personality traits that take from both the Arcturian and Dragon Races.

Starseeds origins and Light Language are a fascinating subject, and much more complex than online "Starseed Trait" lists would suggest. We gave literally devoted our life to researching and teaching the intricacies of various Light Languages. However, you don't have to go that much in depth to discover your own Starseed origins. All you need to do is listen and feel the resonance with the various Star Nations energies. There are resources called the Light Language Libraries. They contain samples of different Light Language types — mostly of Galactic Origins like the (Arcturian, Pleiadian, Sirian, Andromedan, Lyran Feline, Lyran and Avian, Orion, Blue Avian (Azurites) but also ancient Lemurian, Atlantean, Mayan and some others such as the Akashic Language Light Language, Faerie Light Language and the Dragon Light Language.

Information By: **Riya Loveguard – Medium, Ileana Ka**

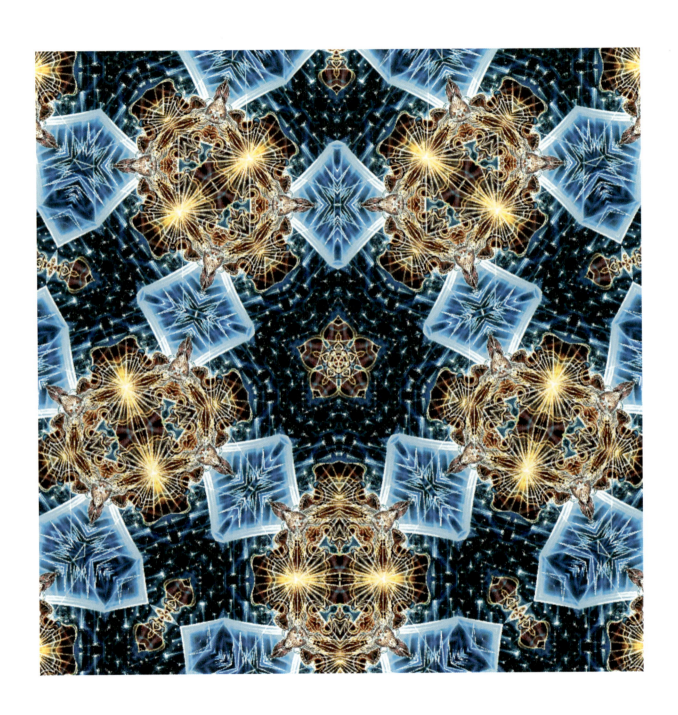

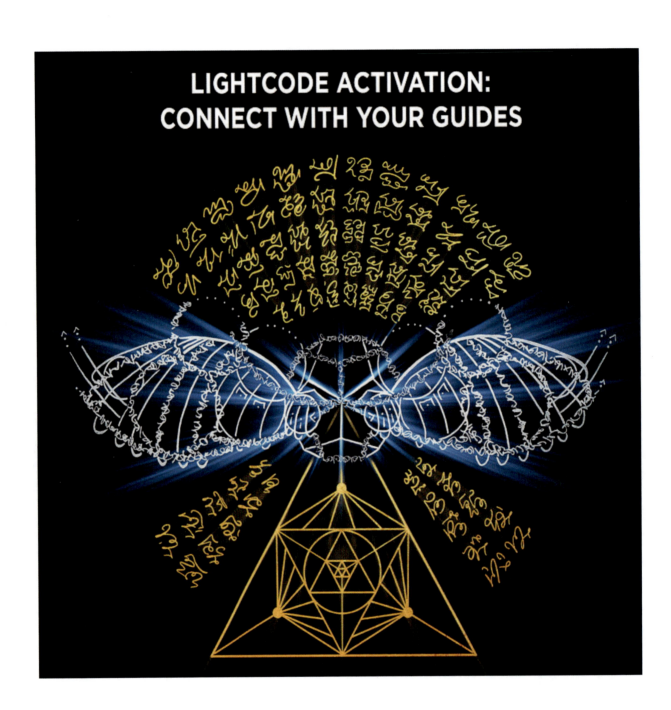

245

Galactic Healing Grids with Crystals

When crystals are put in specific healing grid designs and patterns this can create vibrational intent for healing, prosperity, manifestation and overall raising ones frequency to raise soul consciousness and to increase life force energies to reach higher densities of both body and soul evolution.

Many crystals have both healing and metaphysical properties depending on their colors, sizes, and frequencies so putting crystals on sacred geometry designs or patterns can create positive outcomes for healing as well as manifestation in what you would like to create in your world.

Certain types of crystals have galactic origins like Moldavite which is formed from star energy and then when that material ends up on planets there is a process of volcanic activity that forms it into glass and silicates of various green colors with transformational energetic properties for both healing and metaphysical uses. When these types of crystals are combined in the galactic healing grids it creates a powerful alchemical sequence of soul rejuvenation and a spiritual growth cycle of the body and mind expansion in raising your energetic frequencies for healing and positive manifestation for improving your life journey.

Here are some examples of galactic crystals grids with Moldavite, Labradorite, and Aqua Aura Quartz crystals in the grids that is designed to create powerful properties of healing, spiritual expansion and manifestation.

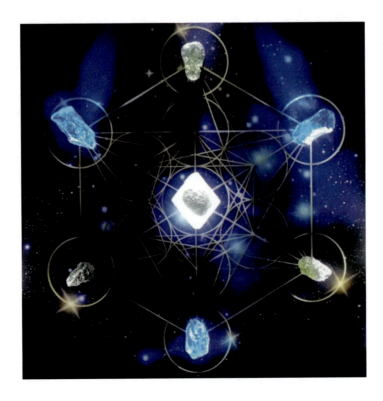

Moldavite Meaning: Physical, Mental, & Spiritual Benefits

Moldavite is a vitreous silica rock that can be found in dark green color and blue-green. It comes under the category of glass and was formed by a meteorite impact 15 million years ago. Moldavite is a form of tektite and is a 5.5-7 on the Mohs hardness scale. The meaning of Moldavite is transformation, fortune, and protection.

Crystals are fascinating. Born under the wildest conditions possible, they often arrive on our mortal plain from fiery volcanoes, shifting rock, surging surf, and starry impacts. Moldavite is no exception. This beautiful rare gem comes from an impact of a meteor with mother earth. It is a byproduct of another place and another time, something that has traveled far and wide to land earth side and be with us in the here and now. Who couldn't be intrigued by this deep green mysterious rock? Moldavite is a one-of-a-kind crystal and we wanted to delve a little deeper to uncover all those mysterious qualities and to find out what extraterrestrial energies this glimmering green gem carries with it.

We are going to take a look at:

- All the healing properties of Moldavite
- Which chakras and zodiac signs it links to
- How to activate your Moldavite gem
- Crystals that make a perfect match for Moldavite
- How to use your Moldavite crystal

If the Moldavite stone feels too overwhelming and you want to start with a simpler stone instead crystals like Citrine, Carnelian, Rose Quartz, and Tourmaline are good to start working with for healing and manifestation.

The Stone of Transformation

- Made by a meteorite colliding with earth
- Found in the Czech Republic
- Highly spiritual and energetic

For almost 15 million years Moldavite has made its home here on Mother Earth. Born from a meteorite that is believed to have crashed into the Bohemian plateau (AKA the modern-day Czech Republic), the impact was believed to have been so fierce that it smashed straight through and into the earth's core leaving pieces of molten rock scattered for miles. Later this rock hardened into Moldavite - a rare forest green gem that can be found along the Moldau River. As Moldavite has been with us for millions and millions of years, it has passed through the hands of our ancestors. Even as far back as Neolithic times, Moldavite was used as a good luck stone especially when it came to matters of fertility. Archaeologists have found cutting tools alongside Moldavite amulets dating back to 25,000 BC out in Eastern Europe. And to this very day, we still adore Moldavite for the magic it can bring us.

There was also a rumor that Moldavite was the stone of the Holy Grail (although it's also believed to be emerald instead). But as the Holy Grail was known to be a stone that rejuvenated people and helped them to heal, it stands to reason that it could be Moldavite as this life-giving gem also shares those same qualities.

Because it literally fell from the stars, Moldavite is highly respected and revered in the spiritual community. It has an intense frequency and even when touching it you can feel this energy surge right through. It's a stone that certainly turns up the dial when it comes to accelerating spiritual and emotional journeys and this can take some getting used to. As Moldavite is earth and stardust infused, it is genuinely a stone of transformation and can bring out some incredible changes in those who know how to harness its otherworldly energy.

Moldavite is rare, precious, and can be pricey because so much of it still sits too deep in the earth. Extracting Moldavite is complex work and refining it is also a delicate job which makes it even more special. Moldavite isn't here en masse and it's likely to go extinct as there is only a limited supply of it on our planet.

Healing Properties

Many believe that the olive green and earthly energy of Moldavite was sent to us to help us ascend. There's no denying this gem has big energy and with big energy comes big shifts.

Moldavite has an intensely high frequency and that fact married with its cosmic collisions and its earthly and extraterrestrial vibes make it a strong stone indeed.

Some people when holding Moldavite for the very first time may even experience what is called the Moldavite flush. The green gem can let off an intense warmth which can send a tingling sensation through the body and lead to the wearer or holder becoming light-headed, giddy, and having a big energy shift. For some people of course this can be overwhelming. Moldavite certainly takes some getting used to, but when you have made your connection with it, this gem can take you to places and along paths you didn't even know were possible.

Physical

- Helps with healthy cell turnover
- Strengthens the eyes

Moldavite is a stone of sublime transformation and in order to heal and ascend, it helps to know every corner of our body. This green gem helps to illuminate those darkened corners so we can see where we are out of balance and get back on track. It encourages rejuvenation and healing, inviting cells to turnover and to move away from damage. The high vibrations of Moldavite can also help shift blocks which can contribute to ongoing pain and progressive illnesses. Like other green gems, it is also good for strengthening and healing the eyes and sorting gastric ailments too. It is believed that Moldavite can also slow down the ageing process and brighten our mental clarity too.

Mental & Emotional Healing

- Helps transform behaviors
- Encourages the release of negative energy

Guiding us towards new heights, Moldavite plays a huge role when it comes to our mental and emotional healing. It's a stone connected to the heart chakra (like other green stones) meaning that it is always keen to encourage us to open our hearts, let go of negative energy, and practice the art of perfectly messy self-love. Moldavite doesn't do things by halves, this stone is sublime at helping to clear out archaic patterns and ideas in order to guide you to a new place where you can thrive. Moldavite does the deep dive - it goes to places untouched and untethers you from traumas you could have been carrying for many years. While this may seem overwhelming it's important, as only by shining a bright light on hidden corners can we see where we need to heal.

Metaphysical Properties

- Helps awaken psychic abilities
- Connects you to spirit guides

Made of stardust and from places unknown, Moldavite definitely scores big when it comes to metaphysical magic. This gem is said to be an amulet sent to earth to help us ascend. It's a stone that serves the spiritual community well, helping to awaken and strengthen psychic abilities, encouraging people to get in touch with their past life lessons, and connecting you to spirit guides and ethereal beings who can show you the way. Along with opening you up to spiritual forces, this gem can also keep you protected. It shares similar properties to Obsidian with its ability to throw up a force field of positive power to stop any bad vibes and harmful entities from getting through. Other crystals that help with activating psychic abilities in the Third Eye and the Crown Chakra is Aquamarine and Angelite crystals they also have metaphysical properties that work on activating the ability to remember past lives and look into past life events. Aquamarine and Angelite is also good for boosting telepathic abilities for communication.

Chakras

- Balances all the chakras
- Is particularly good for the heart chakra
- Also clears the third eye and the crown

Moldavite affects all the chakras (this stone is all about balance and transformation). Being a gorgeous green gem means that it shakes any blockages out from the heart chakra and encourages uplifting healing. The heart chakra sits in the middle of our breastbone and rules how we connect with other people and ourselves. An open heart chakra is essential for building beautiful levels of compassion, leaning into love and trust, healing old heart wounds, and knowing how to hold our own beautiful boundaries. When we have an open heart chakra we are more likely to nurture healthy relationships and not waste our precious time on those that don't spark joy deep within our souls. The Moldavite crystal also works in harmony with our third eye chakra. This is our gateway to all that glorious inner wisdom and how we learn to trust in ourselves too. By strengthening our sense of self-belief, illuminating our own deepest truths, and keeping us equally earthed and rising to new heights, we can be solid and soaring. When our third eye chakra is open, we can open ourselves up to new ideas, visions, dreams, and creative and spiritual practices. By tapping into that third eye energy, we are also able to access those psychic gifts and to rouse our crown chakra to connect with the cosmos. It's that beautiful blend of cosmic charm and earthly weight that makes Moldavite such a worthy stone to work with.

Zodiac sign

- Good for all birth signs

Moldavite is not a traditional birthstone meaning that all zodiac signs can make the most of this glimmering green and transcendental gem. As it is born from the stars, it carries energy for each zodiac sign within its power. It can be a beautiful stone for those born under the banner of spring as it is a crystal that welcomes renewal, freshness, rebirth, and total transformation - all the themes that flourish under the title of new life.

How to Activate Moldavite

- Activate by cleansing, energizing, and programing
- Can be a strongly energetic stone

For those wondering how to activate Moldative, there is a process that involves cleansing, energizing, and programming. The aim is to get the stone cleansed and ready so that you can sync up your energies and program it with your intention. This can be as simple as sitting with it and having it be held in your hand but for those who may be sensitive to the energy of Moldavite, it may take a little more mental work. As mentioned, Moldavite can be a powerful stone and you may experience the flush, this isn't something to fear but you may need to take a break from the stone or balance it with other crystals.

The Activation Process

All crystals can totally benefit from a simple activation process. This is how we sync up energy and transfer intention. This doesn't have to be a big spiritual song and dance, it can be as simple as clearing your mind and your heart and sending it your requests. You may not be the kind of person who wants to send their stone an intention, preferring instead to be led by the universe. While this can be awesome and we applaud the ride, there are people out there who want to be in the driver's seat and who have a specific idea, goal, or manifestation in mind. This is where setting intentions and programming your crystal can certainly help. You may have a big reaction to Moldavite or you may not - either way, you can be sure that this stone is going to be welcoming wonderful changes into your life.

Cleansing

One of the most important steps when setting up your life with any kind of crystal is to get it cleansed and charged up and ready for use. This is a good step to take as you don't know where your gem has traveled from or what energy it has picked up along the way. A simple cleanse and charge will wipe the slate clean and prep it perfectly just for you. Here are a few ways in which you can cleanse your Moldavite.

Water - hold your Moldavite under saltwater or spring water for several seconds so it has a chance for all that energy to run away. You can use tap water but any source of water within a natural setting is sure to be more powerful.

Moonlight - Moldavite is born from the space that sits beyond our sky and thus it reacts beautifully to slants of soft moonlight and the tambourine of the stars. Place your Moldavite on a windowsill at night or even plant it in the ground under a full moon and leave it until morning.

Sunshine - You can leave Moldavite under the warmth of sunlight for a couple of hours, keep it out of harsh direct sunlight.

Singing Bowls - Singing bowls can be a beautiful way to cleanse your Moldavite of any collected energy. If you don't have a singing bowl you can also use chanting, tuning forks, and bells to bring those cleansing sound waves washing over your stone.

Smoke - Whether using incense or smudging with sage, Moldavite will react well to passing through healing smoke.

Other Stones - Some crystals out there have huge cleansing energy and will work wonders when placed in the presence of your Moldavite crystal. Selenite and large geodes or quartz clusters are great gems for this.

Energizing

Now you have a cleansed piece of Moldavite, you may want to get it energized and rev up that spiritual engine. Moldavite loves nature and it thrives from being in natural settings. You can get it buzzing and ready for action by placing it in the earth, meditating with it beneath the rustle and breeze of the trees, and generally connecting it with the natural world whether that's spring water, sunshine, starlight, or soil.

Programming

Programming your Moldavite with your intentions will help you to clear the path of obstacles, balance the chakras, and manifest the life you want to live. Programming your Moldavite stone can be as simple as holding it in your left hand. Our left hand is our receiving hand and our right is our giving hand. As you are asking Moldative and the universe to help you receive that which you desire, it makes sense to use the left hand. Close your eyes, take deep cleansing breaths, and use the power of visualization to envision what it is you want from your Moldavite stone. Be very clear in the asking and try to steer away from ambiguity and stick to specifics. You don't have to just choose one thing from your Moldavite stone, you can ask for all that your heart desires. It may take the body and the mind some time to adjust to the big energy of the Moldavite stone. On the first hold and when programming you may experience tingling, a sense of overwhelm, a high heat running through the body, and you may feel dizzy or lightheaded. This isn't to say you should stop using the stone but tread gently until you have adjusted to its power. This may take some time and you may find yourself a little more tired than usual for a while as your own energy runs to keep up with Moldavite's walk. Be patient and trust that it will fall into the same pace.

Crystals that work with Moldavite Crystal

As mentioned, Moldavite is one of a kind and has big energy. It's not afraid to delve into your shadow side and its intense vibrations can sometimes sweep you off your feet in a way that feels weird. This is why it's so important to stay grounded when dealing with Moldavite. If you are feeling untethered or unstable, you definitely will need some crystal help to adjust to the meteorite magic of Moldavite. One of the best ways to do this is to wear it or use it alongside a gentle nurturing and grounding stone. For this reason, we think Moldavite is an amazing match for Smoky Quartz. If you need a little extra support while delving into the dark corners of your shadow self it helps to have a little more love in the room. Self-compassion is a must when working through the hard stuff and for this reason, we think Rose Quartz is going to bring that soft mothering that is needed. Keeping clear-headed cool energy and overall balance and clarity is also a great match for Moldavite as it stops you from getting zonked out or falling into overwhelm when working with this stone. Clear Quartz is definitely your cheerleader on this front. The Herkimer Diamond is also known to effectively balance the energies of Moldavite too. You can also turn to Amethyst if you want to stay serene and calm and checked in with your crown chakra while working on your spiritual growth with Moldavite.

Using Your Moldavite Crystal

So now you have Moldavite in your life, what is the best way to call on the healing powers of this crystal? One of the best ways to raise your vibrations with Moldavite is to wear it. Moldavite jewelry is an active decision to keep its presence with you when you step out the door. Having Moldavite pressed against the skin is an authentic way to sync up energies all while keeping yourself surrounded by the proactive powers of this precious and rare gem. For those who want to use Moldavite to tap into psychic powers, then meditating with it will help you to access spirit guides, cosmic connections, universal truth, angels, and ancestors too. It is a great gem to have beside you when going through shamanic journeys, past life exploration, and other such spiritual ventures. For those who are keen to clear their heart chakra, you can place Moldavite on that area during meditation. Having your Moldavite close by while journaling or playing with creativity can also help you to remove any kinds of blocks. It's a great tool for elevating consciousness and exploring secret corners of ourselves. There is a lot of healing to be gained from creative work.

We don't recommend keeping Moldavite close to your bed while sleeping as it is such a strong energy stone that its vibes could disrupt your rest patterns. It can be used for those who are delving into lucid dreaming though. Some have said that Moldavite does help with resetting damaged brain patterns for better sleeping but only if you have worked your way up towards using this stone so its energies cannot overwhelm you during sleep nor disrupt your sleep patterns.

Sleeping with Moldavite Under the Pillow

Moldavite is one of the most transformative stones there is. This stone changes you from the inside out, and clears away anything that is in the way of your highest path.

Is It Safe to Sleep with Moldavite?

Sleeping with Moldavite can be very beneficial, but only if you have worked your way up towards using this stone.

Moldavite is a very powerful crystal that holds a very high frequency.

Because of this, anyone who uses Moldavite will experience a transformation in their life.

If you're not used to crystal energy, Moldavite may not be the best stone to sleep with.

But, you can always try it out on your own and see if you can handle it.

If you can, there are many benefits from sleeping with Moldavite.

What Are the Benefits of Sleeping with Moldavite?

Moldavite can help you attune to a new way of being when you use it to sleep.

At night, you are more susceptible to influence, which can be helpful when working with Moldavite's energy.

Are you someone who needs an extreme change in your life?

Or maybe you aren't able to get to a place that you're satisfied with financially.

Moldavite can help you with all of these things.

Emotionally

Sleeping with Moldavite will help you to purge negative emotions. These emotions may be released through your dreams.

If you experience nightmares, this is your body letting go of negative emotions and energy.

Moldavite helps you answer these questions:

"What is holding me back in life?"

"What is truly possible for me?"

"How can I move into the next stage of my life?"

Spiritually

Moldavite is great for connecting you to your spiritual path. This stone releases any roadblocks, blockages or internal energy that may keep you from awakening to your spiritual journey.

Keeping Moldavite around you will help bring a better understanding of the world and yourself.

Life may begin to feel much different than before.

Physically

You can feel a sense of strength and stamina sleeping with Moldavite. You'll have more willpower and maybe even overcome some health challenges that you haven't been able to conquer.

If you work out, Moldavite can help you to have better workouts and increase your physical fitness.

Where Should You Place Moldavite When Sleeping?

You can put Moldavite wherever you want at night.

The energy of these crystals is so powerful that you may not be able to sleep if it's near you at first.

Your dreams may be more vivid, or you may not be able to sleep at all until you're used to this crystal energy.

Our favorite places for keeping Moldavite in our bedroom are:

- Under the pillow
- Underneath the bed
- Inside our wallet while we sleep for prosperity
- On a piece of jewelry

Three-Step Ritual for Placing Your Crystals Under Your Pillow

You should always perform a simple ritual before using your Moldavite at night. Doing so will help increase the properties and high vibrational energy of this crystal.

Hold the Moldavite in your hands for a few minutes to get used to its high vibrational energy. Hold it until you feel attuned to the energy. If you feel energized, uncomfortable, or fearful, continue holding it until these feelings go away. Imagine what you want the Moldavite to help you achieve. See it happening within your mind as if it's happening right now, and charge the crystal with those desires. Place the Moldavite under your pillow. If you are unable to sleep, put it next to your bedside or somewhere in your room.

How Does Moldavite Affect Dreams?

Sleeping with Moldavite can affect your dreams by helping you experience extreme insight and clarity.

Your dreams may be chaotic if you have a lot of unresolved emotions within you.

You may have nightmares as these emotions purge from your energy.

Moldavite can also provide you with inspiration in your dreams that can help you in your waking life.

How to Meditate with Moldavite?

When you think of meditation, you may think of laying on your back for hours on end, not thinking or feeling anything. Well, this isn't how you should meditate with Moldavite. Here's how:

Cleanse your Moldavite using sage or Palo Santo if possible. Hold your Moldavite in your hands and get connected to the energy. Try to feel the energy in your hands as it radiates into your being. Think about all that you want the crystal to help you with. Imagine its healing energy pouring into your life. Now that you've charged your Moldavite, it's ready to be used throughout your day.

You're all set!

Can You Put Moldavite in the Bedroom?

Yes, you can put Moldavite in your bedroom. But, you may not want to until you've spent enough time around it.

This crystal is very high frequency and can be too powerful for some people at first.

Once you spend time with it, you'll get more comfortable with its power.

Some of our favorite places to keep Moldavite in our bedroom are:

- Under the pillow
- On the windowsill
- On the nightstand

What crystals should not be in your bedroom?

While you can technically keep any crystal you want in your bedroom, not all crystals may be beneficial. For instance, crystals that are powerful and have high-frequency energy, such as Moldavite, you may not be able to handle the properties throughout the night.

Other stones that you may not want to sleep with are:

- Diamonds
- Bumblebee Jasper
- Pietersite
- Aura Quartz
- Super Seven

It's up to you to decide which crystals work best in your bedroom. Everyone will have a different experience, especially if they have different needs and intentions for the crystals.

Test them out and see what works best for you!

Moldavite is a powerful stone that can transform your life in amazing ways. If you're not ready for a complete transformation, there are other crystals which you can use for creating healing, protection, and manifestation in your life.

Geological Properties of Moldavite Rock

Chemical Classification	Tektosilicate
Chemical Formula	$SiO_2 + Al_2O_3 + Fe_2O_3$
Crystal System	Amorphous (formerly thought to be from the Moldavite Group of the Tetragonal System)
Color	Green, brownish-green, grayish-green, yellowish-brown
Streak	White
Luster	Vitreous
Transparency	Transparent to translucent
Occurrence	Moldova, Czech Republic, and surrounding areas in Central Europe
Formation	Formed from a meteorite impact about 15 million years ago
Diaphaneity	Transparent to translucent
Cleavage	None
Mohs Hardness	5.5
Specific Gravity	2.32-2.38
Diagnostic Properties	Green color, teardrop shape, bubbly texture
Chemical Composition	Silicon dioxide, aluminum oxide
Crystal System	Amorphous
Optical Properties	Uniaxial negative

Refractive Index	1.48-1.52
Birefringence	0.008-0.013
2V angle	50-70 degrees
Dispersion	0.013
Other characteristics	Tektite, Impactite, found in Czech Republic and Germany

Final Thoughts

Moldavite may not be a beginner stone but it is definitely a good investment for those looking to leap higher and further in a quicker time. That's not to say that there are shortcuts in healing, but for those ready to do the work, Moldavite doesn't beat around the bush. This is a gem that doesn't allow you to sink into stagnancy or skip out on your full potential. It's a stone that doesn't just acknowledge that you want to make a change but one that goes ahead and gets you on the road to do just that. Moldavite is a rare and magical experience.

Moldavite is a powerful crystal that can be both enchanting and overwhelming.

Moldavite FAQs

What does Moldavite do?

Moldavite is a stone of transformation. This fascinating gem has been here for more than 15 million years and is believed to be a great stone for bringing about shifts in energy, encouraging us to let go of negative thoughts and feelings, and untethers us from past traumas so we can move forward in life.

How to tell if Moldavite is real?

Real Moldavite will usually have a mossy color to it rather than a loud and bright green. It will also have inclusions as a clear Moldavite is very rare to find. A true piece of Moldavite will also have various textures going on - it can be smooth and lumpy in parts. It also appears matte rather than slick looking.

What is Moldavite used for?

Moldavite is used for welcoming shifts in energy. It can be an amazing healing gem as it encourages us to work through traumas and tired patterns so we can make space for better things to come. It also helps with themes of self-love, building connection, and can even help to strengthen spiritual gifts and psychic awareness.

How to activate Moldavite?

Moldavite is a big energy stone so you will want to activate it first. You can do this by prepping the stone through a cleansing and charging process. Once cleansed and charged, sit with Moldavite in your left hand and take a few cleansing breaths. Then, use the power of visualization to help you program the stone to help you achieve your dreams.

How to cleanse Moldavite?

Cleansing Moldavite will help it to work at the top of its game and will prevent it from getting blocked or backed up with bad energy. To cleanse it you can use a range of techniques including water, moonlight, singing bowls, and the use of smudging.

How to use Moldavite?

Moldavite can be a very strong stone to use so we recommend building up to it. Once you are used to its energy, you can wear Moldavite jewelry to keep your energy synced and to always be surrounded by protection. You can also use Moldavite on your heart chakra to cleanse the space and welcome in love and compassion. Moldavite can also be used in creative or spiritual practice as it's a gem that sparks cosmic connection and shamanic exploration.

What is Moldavite good for?

Moldavite is an amazing stone for many things and works across the physical, emotional, and spiritual avenues. Physically it's good for shifting blocks that can cause ongoing illnesses. Spiritually it's good for clearing away old patterns so new ones can thrive, and metaphysically it can help with clearing the heart chakra and awakening and strengthening psychic abilities.

What is a Moldavite?

Moldavite is a fascinating stone. It's a vitreous silica rock that came into being after a meteorite impact over 15 million years ago. It falls under the category of glass and usually has a dark green or olive color. Moldavite is known to be a stone of transformation and can help with shifting thoughts and patterns along with protecting you from negative energy.

Can Moldavite get wet?

Moldavite scores between a 5 and 7 on the Mohs hardness scale. It is a relatively tough stone that is born from stardust and as it falls under the category of glass, water shouldn't cause too much damage. However, as with all previous gems and crystals, we don't recommend leaving it in water for extended periods of time.

Is Moldavite dangerous?

Moldavite isn't considered to be a dangerous stone in the physical realm but it can be a very powerful stone spiritually. Some people may feel overwhelmed the first time they hold or wear Moldavite. They may feel light headed or experience a tingling sensation. This is because Moldavite has a high frequency. If Moldavite makes you feel overwhelmed you can start small and build up when using this stone.

Where does Moldavite come from?

Moldavite comes directly from the stars which is why it has such a high frequency and comes with potent and powerful vibes. As it was formed when a meteorite hit Earth 15 million years ago it is only found in the Czech Republic although some pieces can be found in Austria and Germany.

How to charge Moldavite?

Moldavite has a lot of energy but that doesn't mean that it doesn't benefit from a quick charge every once in a while. You can charge it the usual way - moonlight, sunlight, other crystals, etc. but it also likes to be placed among nature so feel free to place it in the earth or under trees.

Where is Moldavite found?

99% of Moldavite is found in the Bohemia area around the Vltava River in the Czech Republic as this is where the crater of the meteorite hit when it fell to Earth 15 million years ago. Some pieces of Moldavite can also be found around Dresden in Germany and near Radessen in Austria.

Where to get Moldavite?

Moldavite is a relatively rare gem but you should still be able to source it from any good crystal seller or a company that deals in geological wonders. Always make sure that you buy from a reputable seller to ensure that the Moldavite you get is the real deal.

How to spot fake Moldavite?

Fake Moldavite may be too vibrant in color and shiny whereas real Moldavite will have a darker green hue going on and will also have a matte look to it. True Moldavite also has inclusions and even sometimes gas bubbles beneath the surface. If your Moldavite is too clear it is probably not the real deal.

Why is Moldavite so expensive?

As much of Moldavite is still buried in the earth and you can only source it from one particular area of Europe it means that this stone can be expensive. Digging Moldavite out of the ground also takes a lot of time and patience and in its raw form it is also found in small droplets rather than big pieces. All of this adds to the cost and worth of Moldavite.

Is Moldavite toxic?

There is nothing within Moldavite that would make it toxic and physically there is nothing worrying about this crystal. Spiritually Moldavite has big energy and can be very powerful which some people can find overwhelming.

Does Moldavite work?

Moldavite is said to be one of the most powerful stones out there. For those who are new to this gem it can cause tingling or overwhelm at the beginning. However, despite its big energy it is a great stone for healing as it can effectively shift patterns, clear out negative energy, and encourage positive change and deep healing.

Is Moldavite a crystal?

Moldavite actually falls under the category of glass and is a type of tektite. This is because it was formed when a meteor hit the Earth 15 million years ago creating the necessary high temperatures and high pressure that is needed for this deep green stone to grow.

How does Moldavite work?

Moldavite has a high frequency and therefore holds a lot of energy. It's been on the Earth for millions of years and was formed by a meteor crashing down from the cosmos. Because of all this, Moldavite carries the energy of shift, change, and even spiritual healing. It works by raising your own vibrations and clearing out blocks from the heart chakra along with inviting you to let go of old traumas and patterns so you can move into a more positive space.

What does real Moldavite look like?

Real Moldavite is usually a darker green color - with hues like moss or olive. It has a matte finish usually rather than looking shiny, slick or wet. It can have varying textures - even on the same piece - ranging from smooth to bumpy and waved. Real Moldavite will also have inclusions beneath the surface along with swirls and bubbles.

Does Moldavite need to be recharged?

Yes, all energetic stones and crystals benefit from a recharge every now and then. As Moldavite is a dab hand at clearing out negative energy, you can keep it clear and working at the top of its game by charging it every once in a while. You can charge Moldavite with moonlight, sunlight, other stones, or even by leaving it under trees, in soil, and close to any kind of plant life.

How is Moldavite formed?

Moldavite was formed when a meteor hit the Earth 15 million years ago. This major impact created the necessary climate for the mossy glass to form - bringing both high pressure and high heat together. The melting and cooling of the silica sand or rock leftover from the impact formed the tektite known as Moldavite.

Is Moldavite rare?

Moldavite is a rare gemstone. As it can only legally be mined in one place in the Czech Republic, there isn't a lot of it on the market and what is already out there is dwindling. All of this adds to the cost of Moldavite and makes it a very special stone to have.

How to use Moldavite to manifest?

If you want to use your Moldavite for manifestation you can sit with the stone in being held in your hand. Take a few cleansing deep breaths and visualize what it is you truly want. Be specific. Now, imagine yourself achieving what it is you want and all the feelings that accompany it. Sit in those feelings for a moment before thanking the stone.

How to work with Moldavite?

There are many ways to work with Moldavite. You can wear the stone in jewelry form for constant protection and healing. You can use it in manifestation or when nurturing spiritual practices and gifts. You can also use it when cleansing the heart chakra. It is recommended to tread gently with Moldavite until you are used to its powerful energy.

Is Moldavite radioactive?

No, there have been no findings of radioactivity present in any Moldavite stones.

How rare is Moldavite?

Moldavite is a very rare gemstone. Because it was born from a meteor collision 15 million years ago, the conditions in which it forms are also quite rare. Moldavite can also only be mined in one village in the Czech Republic (the site of the crash) and getting it out of the earth is quite a delicate job. All of this adds to the stones' rarity and wonder.

How to meditate with Moldavite?

If you want to meditate with Moldavite you can hold it in your hand while you practice letting go of those monkey mind thoughts. You can also lie down and place it on your heart chakra space when meditating to cleanse any blocks and to build on your levels of self-love and compassion.

How to wear Moldavite?

If you want to communicate with higher powers or keep Moldavite in constant connection with your heart chakra you can wear it as a pendant. A Moldavite bracelet will also work by connecting to your pulse and surrounding you in positive energy. A Moldavite ring worn on the index finger can also help you strengthen your intuition whereas worn on the middle finger will help bring out your inner extrovert.

Information By: **Tiny Rituals, Charmed Crystal**

Moldavite Healing Properties, Meanings, and Uses

Quick Overview of Moldavite

Pronunciation

Moldavite mol'də vit'

Color

Green

Chakra Healing

- Crown Chakra
- Third Eye Chakra
- Heart Chakra

Properties

Transformation • Change • Protection • Good Luck • Good Fortune

Moldavite Meanings and Introduction

One look at Moldavite and there's no question it is a stone of greatness, etherically carved of spiritual fire and destined for purpose. This mysterious green talisman is star-born, formed from nature's violent meteoric impact with Mother Earth. Etched by force and flame as it fell from the heavens Moldavite returned to the earth's surface transformed, a glass of amazing delicacy and grace ready to serve humankind.

As a Stone of Connectivity, Moldavite carries an intense frequency, a fusion of earthly and extraterrestrial energies that are quickly felt, often dramatically in those who resonate with its power. Holding Moldavite for the first time often produces a sensation of heat, felt first in the hand, then progressively throughout the body.

In some cases, the Heart Chakra is activated, experienced as a pounding pulse, followed by sweating or flushing of the face, and an emotional release that may range from laughter to tears. Moldavite's frequency may take some getting used to, but its profound ability to accelerate one's personal and spiritual evolution makes it highly sought after in the metaphysical world, both for its life-altering capabilities and as a catalyst for drawing in Light to aid in Earth's healing.

Moldavite is a member of the Tektite group of natural glasses formed from interplanetary collisions. From the Greek word tektos, meaning "molten". Tektites are glassy mixtures of silicon dioxide, aluminum oxide, and other metal oxides with an amorphous crystal structure. Unlike other Tektites from around the world, which are tar black or brownish-black, translucent Moldavite is a deep forest green and is the only variety suitable for cutting and faceting as a gem.

"Moldavite healing has a rich history, prized since the Stone Age as not only a tool but also as a spiritual talisman and amulet of good fortune, fertility, and protection."

This beautiful stone is rare, found only in the Czech Republic and Slovakia, formally known as Czechoslovakia which was disbanded in 1993. While scientists differ in theories regarding Moldavite's origin, nearly all agree its formation coincides with the crash of a large meteorite approximately 14.8 million years ago in what is now the Bohemian plateau.

The rock metamorphosed by the heat of impact, creating a strewn field of Moldavite in the two, mostly rural, areas of Bohemia and Moravia. Farmers often turned up the stones when plowing their fields, while other specimens worked their way to the surface after spring thaw or heavy rains in the fall. More recently collectors have "mined" for gem grade and museum quality specimens by sifting and digging through loose sands and gravels.

Moldavite has a rich history, prized since the Stone Age, and used not only for arrowheads and cutting tools but as a spiritual talisman and amulet of good fortune, fertility, and protection. It was found in the archeological site of the Venus of Willendorf, the oldest known Goddess statue. It has been linked to legends of the Holy Grail, thought to be an Emerald that fell from the sky out of Lucifer's crown before he was cast from Heaven. In Czech lore, it was given as a betrothal gift to bring harmony to marital relations, and for centuries has been used in jewelry, religious items, and spiritual transformation.

Moldavite Appearance

The shapes of Moldavite give witness to its molten origins, most commonly drop-like (round to very flattened), plate or disc-shaped, oval, spheroid, dumbbell-shaped, elliptical, rod-like, or spiral, all common in splash patterns of liquids. Moldavites from Bohemian localities are more drop-like, elongated, or rod-like, while Moravian stones are more spherical. Moldavite occurs most often in shades of deep forest green, though some are pale green or olive, and others, especially from Moravia, are greenish-brown.

The most magnificent of Moldavite's features is the beautifully etched, carved, wrinkled, or sculpted patterns inherent in raw and unpolished stones. Pieces found at or near the surface have been subjected to erosion in streams and rivers over the millennia and resemble the rough exterior common to river stones. More finely textured and sculpted specimens are found in sand or gravel pits. Ones found intact and unmarred are considered "museum-grade" and are both rare and valuable. The rarest of all (less than one percent) are the "sonorous" Moldavites, called Angel Chimes. These are tempered naturally and if dropped on a glass or metal surface they ring like a coin. Moldavite is relatively fragile and should never be cleansed with salt to avoid scratching its surface.

Healing Benefits Overview

Moldavite is good for counteracting cynicism and connects even the most world-weary adult with the wonders of the universe. It eases away doubts, even when the cause is unknown, and calms worries about money by providing solutions not previously considered. Carrying or wearing Moldavite in jewelry allows its energies to remain in one's vibrational field throughout the day strengthening its effects and increasing the incidents of beneficial synchronicities in daily life. Because of Moldavite's intense vibration, some may experience light-headedness or a lack of grounding and may need to acclimate themselves gradually to wearing it.

Moldavite is a useful stone for star children and sensitive souls who find it difficult being in incarnation on the Earth, and who cannot adjust to suffering and deep emotions. Placed on the heart, Moldavite uncovers the reasons and purpose for why one is here and eases the "homesickness" for those whose origin is not Earth.

Moldavite works extremely well in combination with other stones, particularly with the crystalline energies of Quartz varieties. It is one of the Synergy Twelve stones and is ideal for use in making energy tools. Add to wands, headbands, templates, grids, and other devices to intensify their effects.

Moldavite is a powerful aid for meditation and dream work, as well as increasing one's sensitivity to guidance, intuition, and telepathy, and the ability to understand messages sent from the higher realms.

Healing Properties

Moldavite healing properties can help with physical, emotional, and spiritual balance and issues. It has healing powers to help with physical ailments and emotional issues. It is also used in Energy Healing and Chakra balancing. Moldavite healing crystal therapies include slowing the aging process, awakening latent memories, and balancing the Heart Chakra. The therapeutic uses of Moldavite have a long and well-documented history. Meditation with Moldavite is also highly recommended.

Physical Healing Properties

Moldavite is useful as a tool for diagnosis, illuminating the cause and source of an imbalance or disease, and then supports the releasing and healing process. Its high vibrational energy helps re-establish the blocked areas, encouraging the cells to return to their original state of perfection. A rejuvenating stone, Moldavite stimulates personal fulfillment and slows down the aging process. It aids in memory retention and protects against mental degeneration. It may help balance disturbances in the electrical impulses of the brain and is supportive for hard-to-treat progressive illnesses. Moldavite is an excellent stimulant for treating gout, and like many green stones is good for the eyes. It may be beneficial in treating asthma and other diseases of the respiratory tract, allergies, or rashes caused by modern chemicals or pollution, and assisting the body in overcoming the flu and anemia.

Emotional Healing Properties

Moldavite is a stone of the heart, reaching into the deepest inner self and bringing to the surface that which one most needs to recognize, honor, integrate or release. Its resonance brings the heart into union with the mind, allowing them to work together in partnership. The mind in building its creations looks to the heart to see what is worthwhile, and the heart learns to view the self and others with compassion and empathy. The Moldavite crystal is an unconventional stone, inspiring unexpected solutions and awakening latent memories. It assists in releasing archaic belief systems and long-held ideas that no longer serve one's best interests, and has the ability to neutralize hypnotic commands. Those who dislike Moldavite's deep green color often have an aversion to emotion and need to experience unconditional love to find wholeness. They may also have hidden emotional trauma that needs to surface and heal, for which other crystals are required.

Chakra Balancing Healing Properties

Moldavite, with its beautiful green energy, is first and foremost a stone of the heart. However, with its high vibrational frequency, Moldavite's energies can activate any or all of the chakras. This often happens simultaneously and sometimes with great emotional release. It has also been known to stimulate Kundalini energy. The Heart Chakra is located near the center of the breastbone. It regulates our interaction with the external world and controls what we embrace and what we resist. When the Heart Chakra is out of balance you may feel either controlling or controlled in a relationship, and become critical of the little foibles of others, green crystal energy is used to resolve blockages and to re-balance the Heart Chakra, helping us understand our own needs and emotions clearly. Moldavite also stimulates the Third Eye and Crown Chakras. The Third Eye Chakra is the center of our perception and command. It directs our sight and everyday awareness of the world. Our consciousness is located here, and we relate to ourselves through this chakra. When the Third Eye Chakra is in balance our thoughts and internal communications within ourselves are healthy and vibrant. We are open to new ideas, dreams, and can control the flow of energy within all the chakras. The Crown Chakra is located at the top of the head and is our gateway to the expanded universe. It controls how we think, and how we respond to the world around us. It is the fountainhead of our beliefs and the source of our spirituality. When the Crown is in balance, our energies are in balance. We know our place in the universe and see things as they are.

Benefits for Spirituality

Moldavite is a talisman sent to Earth for spiritual awakening, transformation, and evolutionary growth. It facilitates a strong, clear, and direct connection between one's consciousness and the Universal Source. With its own cosmic over soul, Moldavite has an ability to connect with the Ascended Masters, Akashic Records Keepers, Creator Gods and cosmic messengers and draw into the Earth plane those thought patterns and light vibrations that are most beneficial for ascension and illumination in revealing what has been hidden way too long in the shadows now coming into the light to see the reality of creation. Resonating with Moldavite also creates an energy of spiritual protection. It prevents negative energies and entities from connecting with or clinging to one's aura, and assists in disconnecting one from unhealthy personal attachments. Another of Moldavite's important properties is its ability to ground Light for the healing of the Earth. It provides an understanding of the essential unity of all life and our responsibility to see our planet as a whole being in need of love and compassion.

The Color Energy of Moldavite

Moldavite utilizes green color energy and is a "growth crystal" – a powerful conduit of the earth's Life Force of birth, development, and creation, and of the power of nature's constant renewal. It is a potent aid in nurturing, whether of fledgling family relationships or a new business venture. It is perfect for keeping a venture on course, a project on schedule, and life on track. Lighter Green crystals promote spiritual growth and a renewed commitment to a higher purpose. Those of a darker hue are talismans of physical growth, strength, and safety in travel.

Meditation with Moldavite

Meditating with Moldavite may produce powerful visionary states, out of body travel, merging with the Light, or other phenomena. Place it in the hand, on the Heart, Third Eye, Crown, or any Chakra that feels appropriate. It assists in quieting the mind and allows for an easier flow into resonance with the stone's emanating vibrations. Music or guided imagery enhances the experience. Since meditation with Moldavite raises the consciousness to the highest spiritual dimension, it is important to ground during or after these sessions with stones such as Hematite or Smoky Quartz, or by holding a pair of Boji Stones. Clear Quartz helps stabilize Moldavite's effects.

Moldavite Meanings in Divination

The Divinatory meaning of Moldavite is... A dramatic change in your life for the better.

Crystals and Angels

If your birthday falls in any of the following periods, a Moldavite of the color listed can be a valuable conduit to your Guardian Angel. The table also provides the name of the Guardian Angel of those born in the time period.

Date	Crystal Color	Name of Guardian Angel
Jan 1 - Jan 5	Green	Nemamiah
March 31 - April 4	Dark Green	Sitael (Sirael)
June 6 - June 10	Green	Hakamiah
July 7 - July 11	Light Green	Ieiaeil (Jejalel)
Sept 3 - Sept 7	Green	Yehudiah
Sept 8 - Sept 12	Dark Green	Lehahiah
Dec 27 - Dec 31	Dark Green	Poiel (Polial)

There are other Angels that are partial to Moldavite, too. The table below gives you more information about them.

Purpose	Crystal Color	Name of Angel
Raphael is known as the Glory Angel; Tree of Life, the Angel of Wednesday, the Ruler of Mercury. He is also the Master of Tarot Card 0 "The Fool" and the 1st Tarot Card "The Magician". Raphael also Heals Illness and is the Ruler of The west wind. He is the Angel of Compassion, Knowledge, Progress, Repentance, and Love.	Dark Green	Raphael
Master of the 11th Tarot Card "Justice".	Dark Green	Chadaqiel
Protector and Ruler of the dates Sept.8-12; Virgo.	Dark Green	Lehahiah
Protector and Ruler of the dates December 27-31; Capricorn.	Dark Green	Poiel
Protector and Ruler of the dates March 31- April 4; Aries.	Dark Green	Sitael
The Angel of the Birds.	Green	Arael
Angel of Mercury.	Green	Cochabiel
Protector and Ruler of the dates June 6-10; Gemini.	Green	Hakamiah
Metatron is the Crown Angel, the Tree of Life, and helps to Heal Learning Disorders. He is also the Master of the 20th Tarot Card "Judgment".	Green	Metatron
Protector and Ruler of the dates January 1-5; Capricorn.	Green	Nemamiah
Master of the 18th Tarot Card "The Moon".	Green	Vakhabiel
Protector and Ruler of the dates September 3-7; Virgo.	Green	Yehudiah
Helps to Heal Anxiety and the Angel Tuesday.	Light Green	Chamuel (Khamael)
Protector and Ruler of the dates July 7-11; Cancer.	Light Green	Ieiaeil
Ruler of Earth/Night and the Angel of Conception/Babies Names.	Light Green	Lailah (Lailiel) (Leliel)
Shimshiel or Shamshiel is known as the Ruler of Earth/Day. He is also the Master of the 19th Tarot Card "The Sun".	Light Green	Shimshiel (Shamshiel)

Moldavite for the Goddess

Crystals of Green color honor Persephone, the Greek Goddess of Spring. She represents celebration and the Earth alive with new growth. Moldavite may also be used to honor Gaia, the Greek Earth Mother Goddess. Born directly out of Chaos, the primal emptiness, she was the first (or one of the first) beings to appear during the process of creation and is honored as being the Earth itself.

Moldavite Birthstone

There are several ways to find an appropriate birthstone. The traditional one is listed first. These are from the popular lists that most people are familiar with. The second way is to find your natural birthstone by the color wheel of life. Finally, many people use the traditional stones of the Zodiac.

In this section, you will find information on all three approaches.

Traditional Birthstone

Moldavite is not a traditional birthstone.

Natural Birthstone

Moldavite is one of the natural birthstones of those fortunate enough to be born in the heart of spring (April 20 – May 20).

It will help to bring you renewal, success in new ventures, and good health.

Zodiac Crystal

Though not associated with any specific zodiac sign, Moldavite is a stone born of the stars and is, therefore, a universal product of all the signs.

Meaning in Talismans and Amulets

Dating even into pre-history, Moldavite has always been revered as a spiritual talisman and an amulet for good fortune and fertility. The Neolithic peoples of Eastern Europe wore Moldavite at least 25,000 years ago, and the earliest known goddess statue, the famed Venus of Willendorf, was discovered in a digging site with a number of Moldavite amulets.

Using Moldavite in Feng Shui

Moldavite utilizes Wood Energy, the energy of growth, expansion, new beginnings, nourishment, and health. It enhances vitality, brings abundance, and keeps us growing physically. Use green crystals to enhance any space used for eating, in the room of a small child, or in a place of your home where you are beginning a new project. Wood Energy is traditionally associated with the East and Southeast areas of a home or room. It is associated with the Family and Health area, and the Prosperity and Abundance area.

Meanings in Ancient Lore and History

The green stones from the sky have been prized by humans as far back as the Early Paleolithic period for sharp-edged tools and arrowheads, as well as wearing them as amulets. Some of these amulets were found in the same archeological dig as the Venus of Willendorf, the oldest known Goddess statue, and may have been used to honor her. They were also discovered in layers of strata containing pottery associated with Late Neolithic cultures. In Czechoslovakian folklore, Moldavite was believed to bring good luck and harmony to marital relationships and for centuries was given as a betrothal gift. Throughout the Middle Ages Moldavite was so highly prized only nobility or royalty were allowed to wear it, and in later centuries was quite popular being worn in pendants and as adornments in men's walking sticks. Many specimens reside in various museums and institutions, private collections, and even NASA possesses a number of Moldavites. In the 1960s, the Swiss government gave a gift of Moldavite to Queen Elizabeth II on the tenth anniversary of her coronation, a beautiful naturally sculpted raw stone set in platinum and surrounded by diamonds and black pearls. There was also a rosary of faceted Moldavite beads with a carved Madonna made for Pope John Paul II as a gift from the Czechoslovakian people. "Moldavite has found acclaim as a spiritual relic associated with the legends of the Holy Grail." In the last century, Moldavite has found acclaim as a spiritual relic associated with the legends of the Holy Grail. In recorded history, the Grail vessel was held to be the cup that caught the blood of Christ as He died on the cross. In the Arthurian romances, the Grail cup magically passed among the knights and ladies seated at the Round Table during the feast of Pentecost, giving each the food they most desired – holy nourishment. A drink from the Grail brought healing and rejuvenation, and spiritual awakening. It guided the knights on quests for their right paths of destiny. In some versions, the Grail was the chalice used by Christ at the Last Supper, while others believed the Grail was not a cup, but a stone – an Emerald that fell from the sky out of the crown of Lucifer during the war between God and Satan, and was brought to Earth by angels who remained neutral. The ancients called all the clear green gemstones "Emeralds" and Moldavite is the only such stone to fall from the sky. In other stories, the cup was carved from the Emerald. Some translators interpret the Emerald as being from Lucifer's forehead and not his crown, and have linked this with the pearl fixed in the brow of the Indian god Shiva. Called the Urna, this stone is like the Third Eye that allows one to see inward to knowledge and perfection. "Moldavite is associated with the phoenix, consumed by fire and reborn in fire, a symbol of spiritual renewal." In history an actual "Grail" was discovered and brought to Napoleon, a bowl called the Saint Graal reputed to be a platter used by Christ at the Last Supper. Napoleon, under expert examination, was disappointed to find it was made of green glass. While Moldavite is green glass, there is only speculation as to whether the true bowl might have been substituted to keep it from Napoleon, or whether the bowl was indeed the Grail. Another historically noted chalice made of gold and adorned with Moldavites was used as an ostensory (a vessel in which the consecrated Host is presented for the veneration of the faithful), and was passed down through the centuries but disappeared during the Second World War. Moldavite's Sanskrit name is Agni Mani, meaning "fire pearl". In the 1930s the famed artist and mystic Nicholas Roerich drew a close analogy of Moldavite, the fire pearl, to the Stone of Shambhala, the most sacred jewel of Tibet believed to be of celestial origin from the constellation of Orion, and further asserted it must be the same stone as in the Holy Grail. Moldavite is also associated with the phoenix, consumed by fire and reborn in fire, a symbol of transfiguration and spiritual renewal. It is also referred to as the Philosopher's Stone, the Grail of alchemists, for its qualities of transformation and the bestowal of youth and longevity.

More Crystal Information

What is Moldavite?

Moldavite is a vitreous silica projectile glass.

Where is Moldavite found?

High-quality Moldavite is primarily found in the Czech Republic. Other sources for Moldavite include Germany and Austria.

How is Moldavite formed?

Moldavites are tektites, a natural glass generated by the melting and cooling of silica sand or rock thrown into the sky due to a meteorite impact.

What is Moldavite good for?

Moldavite is good for inciting change, personal growth, transformation, and inspiring unexpected solutions.

Can Moldavite go in water?

Moldavite is safe when being rinsed with water. However, long-term soaking can cause damage. Moldavite is safe to wear in a chlorinated pool or saltwater for short periods.

What does Moldavite mean?

Moldavite is an intense stone of transformation, fortune, and protection.

How do you cleanse Moldavite?

Moldavite can be cleansed using any of the usual cleansing methods. The recommended options are running it through water, using other crystals such as Selenite, or soaking it in sunlight.

How do you charge Moldavite?

Moldavite can be charged using any of the usual charging methods. People have found Vogels to be greatly effective in charging their Moldavite.

Can Moldavite be left in the sun?

Moldavite is safe to be left in the sun.

How hard is Moldavite?

On the Mohs Hardness Scale, Moldavite is a 5.5 - 7.

Why is Moldavite called Moldavite?

Armand Dufrenoy named Moldavite after the Bohemian town of Moldauthein.

How to use Moldavite?

Moldavite is an intense stone to work with. It is highly recommended to work with it in short doses and slowly increase the length of time. Moldavite can be used in many different ways. The most popular uses include jewelry, meditation, carrying it with you, placing it in your home, or in grids. The Moldavite stone is used to create healing, protection, and for manifestation.

What does Moldavite look like?

Moldavite is a transparent or translucent mossy green stone with swirls and bubbles that add to its appearance.

How can you tell if Moldavite is real?

Fake Moldavite can't replicate the old-age appearance that real Moldavite has from being created many years ago. Fake Moldavite will always look wet and shiny new in appearance. No two Moldavites should look similar. Fake Moldavites are made with molds of real Moldavite, and the makers of these Moldavites tend to reuse the same molds and flood the markets with duplicates. Most fake Moldavites come from China or India. Make sure you are shopping from a reputable vendor that knows the origin of the stones. Real Moldavite is full of imperfections and contains air bubbles inside. Fake Moldavite can also have bubbles, but you'll find them on the surface rather than inside.

Why is Moldavite expensive?

Moldavite isn't readily available and it is difficult to extract from the ground because it is basically glass making it delicate. Moldavite is usually extracted by hand versus tools and machinery to avoid damaging the fragments. The demand for Moldavite has recently skyrocketed while the supply for Moldavite is scarce, which drives the cost up.

Information By: **Crystal Vaults**

HOW TO CREATE A CRYSTAL GRID IN 7 STEPS

Whether you're trying to manifest more self-love, a vacation, or a new job, crystal grids can help! Crystal grids can be as simple or complex as you make them and a simple grid can be just as powerful at helping you manifest your goals as a complex one. Think of a crystal grid as your manifesting ally! It may not be the only tool you use to manifest your desires, but it can certainly help.

There are just a few necessary steps you need to follow to create a crystal grid. First, let's briefly discuss why crystal grids work.

WHY CRYSTAL GRIDS WORK

Crystals are formed from perfect geometric patterns and this is one reason why crystals are such a powerful healing tool! The perfect geometry within crystals makes them an ideal energy conduit and easily programmable. By placing several crystals in a repeating grid format, you will amplify their power. Using sacred geometry as a grid template for your crystals adds another layer of perfect geometric patterns to help better communicate your intentions.

If those reasons seem a little too out there for you, view crystal grids as a beautiful reminder of your intention. The most important part of manifesting your desires is visualizing what you want daily, and your crystal grid will serve as a reminder to do just that.

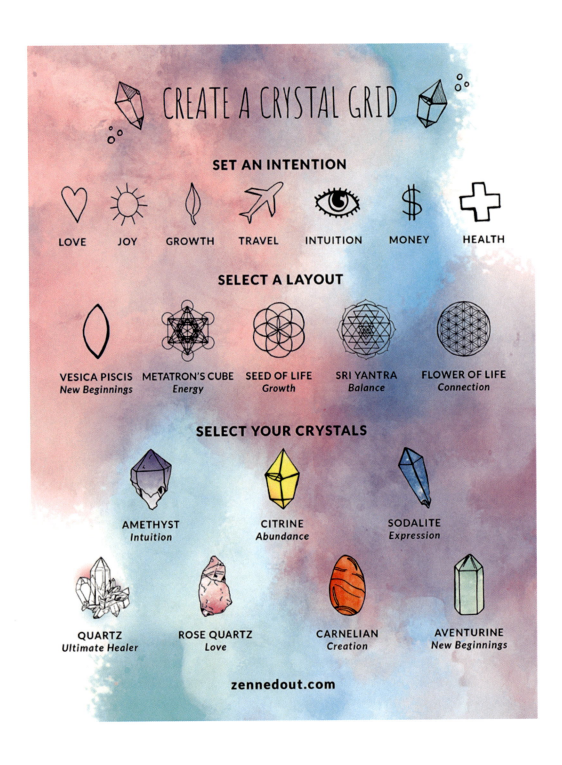

7 STEPS TO CREATE A CRYSTAL GRID

1. SET AN INTENTION

Your intention for your grid is your starting place and will lay the foundation for everything else you choose for your grid. Get quiet and breathe for a few minutes so you can gain complete clarity about what it is you want. Don't play small; you deserve everything you desire! Once you've set an intention for your grid, you can start selecting your grid format and crystals.

2. SELECT YOUR GRID FORMAT

Sacred geometry is an ideal format for crystal grids because it is symmetrical and each symbol carries unique energy that will help amplify your intention. Several different sacred geometry symbols can be used, here's a list of the most common ones and the categories they're best suited for:

- **Vesica Piscis:** Birth, femininity, sexuality, new beginnings, new projects
- **Seed of Life:** Inspiration, potential, chakras, creativity, growth
- **Flower of Life:** Community, connection, love, communication, partnerships, intuition
- **Metatron's Cube:** Cleansing, clearing, balancing, energy, chakras, healing
- **Sri Yantra:** Balance, male energy, feminine energy, meditation, connection to Source Energy

3. SELECT YOUR CRYSTALS

Now, the fun part! Let's select your crystals. A pointed crystal will work well for the center stone, and tumbled crystals work well for the secondary crystals that will radiate around the center stone. You don't need 50 crystals to have a grid that works. Even if you have one center stone and a handful of quartz, you can make an effective crystal grid. Clear quartz is your crystal grid bestie because it is ideal for all intentions, easily programmable, and super amplifying. We suggest using three different stones to strengthen your intention with the addition of five or more pieces of clear quartz.

A quick google search of "crystals to help with _____" will go a long way! However, here are some common crystals and the purposes they're best suited for:

- **Amethyst:** Intuition, calm, peace
- **Citrine:** Abundance, joy, happiness
- **Sodalite:** Creativity, expression, communication
- **Quartz:** Balance, health, cleansing
- **Rose Quartz:** Self-love, compassion, friendship
- **Carnelian:** Sex, creativity, birth
- **Green Aventurine:** New beginnings, wealth, growth

4. CLEANSE YOUR TOOLS AND SPACE

Cleanse your crystals, any other tools you'll be using, and the space you're creating your grid in. You don't want any lingering bad juju playing a role in your manifesting! Cleanse with an herbal smoke of your choice, cleanse under the light of the full moon, or envision a bright white light cleansing your space and tools.

5. SET YOUR GRID UP

You'll want to place your center stone first. You can base your center stone selection on a few things, like a stone that best matches your intentions, the largest stone, or a crystal you have a personal affinity for. Next, place your other stones radiating out around the center stone in a balanced format. As you place each stone visualize your end goal of what you'd like to manifest.

6. ACTIVATE YOUR GRID

Think of activating your grid as turning on the lights. You've set everything up, and now its show time! There's more than one way to activate your grid. The simplest method is to close your eyes and imagine the energy of all of your crystals connecting and communicating your desires to the universe.

You've set an intention and created a beautiful crystal grid, but now what? Activating your crystal grid is a great way to spend more time with it, reinforce your intention, and bring positive energy into it.

As a note, crystal wands are beautiful but they're not a necessity for activating your grid. You can use a point crystal of your choice or even your hand.

"CONNECT THE DOTS" METHOD

Start on the outer crystals of your grid with your crystal wand or a pointed crystal, and start drawing lines between the crystals, just like you'd do for a dot-to-dot drawing. Continue working your way closer to the center, drawing invisible lines between all of the crystals. Once you reach the center stone take a moment to close your eyes and imagine the energy of the stones uniting and connecting.

7. BE PRESENT WITH YOUR GRID DAILY

Don't just set it and forget it! Make sure to take a few quiet moments every day to connect with your grid. Connecting with your grid daily will allow you to visualize your desires and goals.

Leave your grid up for a complete moon cycle, or longer if you'd like. If it does start to attract dust give it a light clean to prevent the energy from stagnating. Find a free printable crystal grid template here.

Information By: **Cassie Uhl**

A Grid For Money

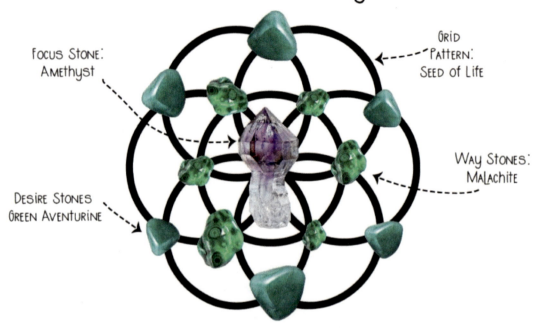

Focus Stone: Amethyst

Grid Pattern: Seed of Life

Way Stones: Malachite

Desire Stones Green Aventurine

Beginners Balancing Grid

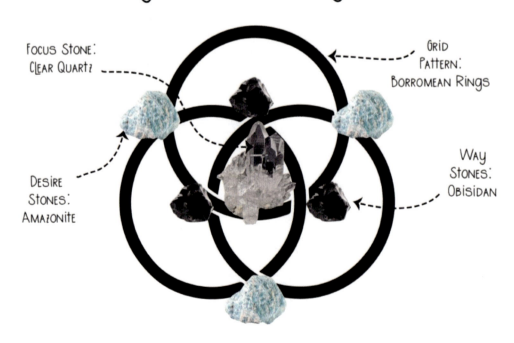

Focus Stone: Clear Quartz

Grid Pattern: Borromean Rings

Way Stones: Obisidan

Desire Stones: Amazonite

Sacred Geometry Symbols

Grounding & Balancing the Physical, Emotional and Soul Divine Energies for healing of the whole soul grid

Have a sacred geometry Symbol in mind that you want to use for your crystal grid base. Each of the symbols have a specific meaning. This is the elemental dragon protection for the grounding and balancing of the physical, emotional, and soul divine energies for healing of the whole soul grid.

Examples of Crystal Grid Types and the Crystals that you would use for the design of your custom crystal grid(s)

Grid Type: Grounding & Balancing the Physical, Emotional and Soul Divine Energies for healing of the whole soul.

Base: Creating the healing energies of grounding and balancing the physical existence, emotional stability and soul divine happiness in one's lifetime.

Crystals Used:

Titanium Quartz: Forty four Titanium quartz points used. Titanium projects strength, elevated mental activity, and fortitude. The Quartz enhances these qualities and will energize the entire chakra system.

Rainbow Titanium Coated Druzy Geode Sphere: One Titanium Coated Druzy Geode sphere. The sphere had a combination of Crystal Quartz and Agate mixed in.

Titanium Aura Quartz: One Titanium Aura Quartz sphere. Titanium quartz amplifies and magnifies healing energy and clears and cleanses chakras. It helps to amplify both body energy and healing thoughts. It is used to enhance creativity. Helps to remove blockages and enhances psychic powers.

How to Create and Use a Crystal Grid

When you jump into the world of gemstone energy, sacred geometry, and manifesting, it can be a little intimidating knowing where to start. There are so many different types of crystals that are all said to harness unique benefits. We are here to share with you that it doesn't have to be complicated! The amazing thing about this world of high-vibes and intention setting is that YOU get to decide how it all works for you.

WHAT IS A CRYSTAL GRID?

Crystal grids are amazing tools to use when you are feeling pulled to call something new into your life. Whether you want to manifest more wealth, love, health, opportunities - the key is simply to declare it. Once you have declared your intention, you are instantly setting things in motion. Adding in a crystal grid to your intention-setting rituals is an incredible way to amplify all your deepest desires.

So, what is a crystal grid?

A crystal grid is a specific arrangement (using sacred geometry) of gemstones to amplify energy for a set intention. As a result, the intention becomes more powerful which allows for easier manifestation to happen. Sacred geometry is based on the principle that all things in the universe follow a predefined shape corresponding to their molecular vibration. These shapes and patterns can be observed in art, music, architecture, and even in the nests, shells, or bones of living things. *How cool is that?* It is also said that these different shapes harness their own power making them ideal in crystal grid formations!

CRYSTAL GRID SHAPES

A few of our favorite shapes that we turned into crystal grids are:

Metatron's Cube Crystal Grid
This symbol represents the journey of energy throughout the universe, and of balance within the universe. This is a great symbol to use when wanting to manifest feelings like patience, happiness, and curiosity.

Seed of Life Crystal Grid
This symbol is the doorway to infinite possibilities. It represents all possible beginnings and paths in life. This pattern can be used for any intention and is especially helpful when working with balance, harmony, truth, protection, creation, and completion.

Flower of Life Crystal Grid
This special symbol represents the cycle of life. It is believed that within this symbol holds the most meaningful and sacred patterns of our universe. This is a great choice if you are wanting guidance or answers in a certain area of your life.

HOW TO USE A CRYSTAL GRID TO ATTRACT ALL THAT YOU DESIRE

Use these guided instructions to help you manifest all that you desire.

STEP ONE:
Choose 3 types of gemstones/crystals that harness the energy of what you want.

In total, you will need 13 stones (1 Focus/Anchor stone, 6 Way stones and 6 Desire stones). Let your intuition guide you. If you are working on an abundance grid and for some reason, you feel drawn to moonstone, trust that and include moonstone in your grid. Alternately, use the stones you have available to you, you don't have to go on a shopping spree to make a powerful and effective crystal grid. Don't stress over this process, just trust your gut and choose stones that you are feeling drawn to.

Focus/Anchor Stone is the one that collects the universal life force and channels it through the grid. **Way Stones** surround the Focus Stone and enhance its energy. **Desire Stones** are the foundation. They gather the energy of the other stones and create strength and power within the grid.

Crystal grids might have symbols on them like suns, moons, hearts, etc. that could have a special frequency meaning connected to soul codes, light codes, soul purpose, soul mission, light language toning of vibrational acoustic meaning that exists within sacred geometry as well as within yourself and it creates a pathway bridge that carries the energetic frequencies of this information within the symbols as well to certain crystals that someone is drawn on a soul frequency that you are called to activate the crystal grid with intention and manifestation. Having an awareness of which type of symbols and crystals you use and what their meaning as well as purpose is can set up the final frequencies of your crystal grids for what you are creating in your reality. Crystals have both healing and metaphysical properties so what is the aim as frequency and energy coming from the crystals to create your manifestation into physical reality in your life existence.

STEP TWO:
Choose the stone that will be your Focus stone. This is the stone that will sit in the center of your grid. It can be larger than the rest and any shape or cut you would like *(standing points make great Focus stones as the energy omits out the very top making it super powerful!)*

STEP THREE:
Grab 6 Way stones and 6 Desire stones. These can be simple, tumbled stones or any other shape you wish just make sure they are not too big or else you might have trouble fitting everything on your grid.

STEP FOUR:
Choose the geometric shape of your grid. Select which one feels best for you trusting that whatever you choose is the perfect one for you.

BUILDING YOUR CRYSTAL GRID

You're now ready to build your grid!

1. Define your intention. What do you want this crystal grid to do for you? Be specific. Write it down. You can place this piece of paper under your grid, fold it up and place it right in the middle of the grid or keep it close to you - in a bag, wallet, or pocket for example.

2. Pick up 6 stones *(make sure they are all the same type)* hold them in your hands. Close your eyes. Spend a few minutes thinking of what you want. Imagine as if the desired outcome is already yours. When you are ready, place the crystals in a symmetrical pattern around the largest part of your grid. Symmetry is key so follow the pattern making sure your stones sit in the same place at equal distances apart.

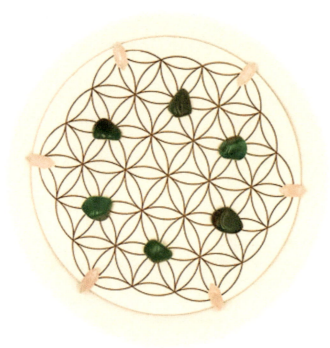

3. Pick up the other 6 stones. Again, close your eyes and think of your intention. When you are ready place these stones in a symmetrical pattern around the center of the grid. Check out these photos for guidance.

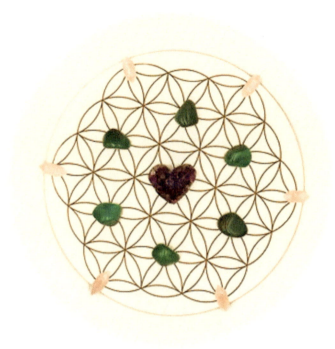

4. Lastly, pick up your Focus stone. You are ready to anchor in your intention. Placing the Focus crystal last is symbolic of involution or "returning to center" and calls in a higher power that allows access to infinite possibility. As you place this stone in the center of the grid, say your intention out loud. Give thanks to your stones for assisting you in your journey. Saying your intention out loud activates your crystal grid.

5. Make time to connect to the energy of your grid regularly. You may want to meditate in front of your grid each day for a few minutes, or just sit in the presence of your grid to fill you up with the energy you're trying to create in your life. Just be sure to hold space in your life for positive changes in whatever form is for your highest good.

That's it! Let the magic happen!

Crystal Meaning: Our Favorite 40 Stones

Every crystal has its own distinct meaning and energetic property. If you feel like your energy is unbalanced, you're going through difficulties either spiritual or physical, or you want to add in a <u>high-vibe tool</u> to your life, you may benefit from the power of crystal/gemstone energy.

Here is a list of crystals - our 40 favorite stones - complete with their meanings. These are our go-to <u>stones to wear</u>, use in crystal grids and keep in our home.

CRYSTAL MEANINGS

Agate is known as a harmonizing stone by stabilizing yin & yang energies. It is said to promote feelings of calm with great strength.

Amazonite is known as a stone of courage and promotes positive action. It is said to help with emotional support specifically balancing high emotions to encourage self-determination.
Amethyst is known for its ability to purify and cleanse the energy in a space. It is said to promote feelings to relieve stress and encourage happiness and joy.

Apatite is known as a stone of manifestation. It is best used when meditating as it assists in clearing frustration and supports high and low emotions.

Aquamarine is known for its ability to calm feelings of overwhelm. It is said to assist in finding the root of a problem, within, to clarify perception.

Aragonite is known for being an excellent grounding stone. It is said to stabilize emotions for people who push themselves too hard and encourages delegating.

Aura Quartz is a process that bonds metals and minerals to quartz. It is said to still possess an intense energy of calmness assisting with relieving negativity and stress promoting joy and optimism.

Black Tourmaline is known for its powerful protective energy. It is said to repel and protect from negativity.

Blue Lace Agate (raw)

Blue Lace Agate is known as a stone to assist with "starting over". It is said to possess a gentle energy that instills peace of mind.

Calcite is known for its assistance in boosting joy and happiness. It is also said to promote feelings of clarity and guidance when making difficult decisions.

Carnelian is known for its assistance in boosting creativity, stamina and motivation. It is said to be an energizing and uplifting crystal.

Celestite has a gentle, calming energy that assists in shifting perspectives allowing for a graceful solution. It is said to give a sense of soothing, uplifting feeling that you are being watched over by a loving caretaker.

Chrysocolla is known to aid in heartache by drawing out negative emotions. It is said to promote healing from within and assist in overcoming past anguish.

Citrine (rough)

Citrine is known as a prosperity stone attracting good luck, fortune, and success. It is said to transform negative energy into a positive form of energy.

Clear Quartz is known as a cleansing and amplifying crystal. It is said to absorb, regulate and release negative energy.

Fluorite is known to draw off negative energies and promotes mental clarity by blocking unwanted mental influences. It is said to stabilize and balance the mind.

Garnet is known as a powerful energizing stone of protection. It is said to inspire love and devotion by opening the heart and boosting self-confidence.

Green Aventurine (polished)

Green Aventurine is known as a stone of renewing one's optimism promoting confidence and happiness. It is also said to be a stone of opportunity and good fortune.

Hematite is a magnetic stone that is known for its grounding and protective energies. It is said to absorb then transform negative energy into positive.

Jade is known as a stone that brings protection and good luck. It is said to harness a gentle energy that harmonizes negative thoughts and promotes positive feelings that attract authentic friendships.

Jasper is known as the "Supreme Nurturer" supporting in all aspects during times of stress. It is said to provide protection by absorbing negative energies and balancing emotions.

Labradorite is known as a stone of transformation and courage. It is said to help banish fears and insecurities during times of change.

Lapis Lazuli (polished)

Lapis Lazuli is known for possessing enormous serenity and protective energies. It is said to harmonize emotions and stimulate the brain for encouraging creative thoughts.

Lava is solidified volcanic material. Being that lava comes from the center of the earth, it is very grounding and protective. It is said to aid in inducing feelings of calm and stability.

Lepidolite is known to dissipate negativity and induce feelings of calm. It is said to have soft, nurturing energies that allow us to connect to our inner being and help love ourselves.

Moonstone is known for its ability to enhance intuition and calm anxiousness. It is said to assist in balancing emotions to help with clear decision making.

Moss Agate is known as a stone of new beginnings by releasing mental and emotional blockages. It is said to aid with intuition and protect vulnerability.

Obsidian (rough)

Obsidian is known for its strong protective energy and grounding abilities. It is said to form a protective shield in a negative environment.

Onyx is known for its powerful protective energies. It is said to help banish old/bad habits and is used to build confidence and strength.

Opalite is a man-made stone of opalescent glass. It is said to assist with increasing self-esteem and self-worth.

Petrified Wood is known for its high grounding vibrations to help with strong feelings of worry. It is said to assist in accepting things that are not able to be controlled and supporting change to things that are able to be controlled.

Pyrite is known as "fool's gold" as it was commonly mistaken for gold. It is an excellent energy shield blocking out negativity. It is said to be a "good luck" stone attracting wealth and abundance.

Rose Quartz is known as a stone that represents universal love. It is said to attract feelings of appreciation with new relationships, deepen existing partnerships and encourages self-love.

Selenite is known for its cleansing and charging abilities. It can cleanse the energy of other stones while also charging them at the same time. It is said that selenite is a stabilizer of emotions and induces clarity of the mind.

Shungite is known for its profound protective and purifying properties. It is said to protect against radiation, electromagnetic and geopathic emissions.

Smoky Quartz is known as an efficient grounding and cleansing stone. It is said to assist with calming anxiety and emotions in times of stress.

Sodalite is known for its ability to bring calmness and clarity to the mind. It is said to encourage rational thought which then brings emotional balance to calm anxiousness.

Tiger's Eye (polished)

Tiger's Eye is known as a protective stone against negativity and negative self-talk. It is said to promote feelings of emotional stability and strength.

Tourmaline is known as a protective stone to purify and transform negative energy into a lighter vibration. It is said to help understand one's self-promoting for boosting self-confidence and diminishing fear.

White Howlite is known for its ability to promote feelings of calm. It is said to assist in dissolving stress and soothe feelings of irritability.

Information By: **Laura McKinnon – Dropsofgratitude**

Crystalline Grid and Gate Keepers

The Earth's Crystalline Grid is a multidimensional grid of the ascended Earth, holding the template for a 5D New Earth.

It is an etheric network of facetted light, portals, vortexes and access points covering the entire Earth's energetic field. The crystalline grid is a network much like the human nervous system, transmitting signals of light frequencies connecting all beings of Earth with multidimensional timelines of Earth's creation, past, present and future. The crystalline grid is the higher dimensional geometric structure anchoring the 5D ascended New Earth consciousness. The crystalline grid connects all beings and our planet with cosmic forces and other dimensional realms. In becoming multidimensional beings, like we were back in Lemuria, we as a collective will align with the crystalline grid, downloading and integrating ascension codes for activating our etheric crystalline light bodies and raising the vibration of Earth to unite in the 5D ascended New Earth paradise.

The crystalline grid is a network for us to tune in to the multidimensional galactic communities here to assist us in ascending to higher dimensions, opening new channels of telepathic communication.

When we sync with the crystalline grid we become activated, a beacon for the network of higher light frequency to transmit through us codes for ascension, amplifying the grid's "broadcast" signal.

We can connect to the planetary crystal grid and download light codes, navigational coordinates and energy maps, essentially the blueprints for Ascension. We can ground these downloads into the physical from the etheric, to integrate the guidance and direction for our mission here on Earth now, to serve the healing and awakening of the planet.

By connecting with the Earth's crystalline grid we can:

- Unite with other Lightworkers and with our star families and spirit guides
- Send love and healing energy to the collective
- Download ascension codes for telepathy and developing our intuitive abilities
- Download codes for assisting in planetary healing
- Assist in raising the vibration of self and others
- Activate our crystalline light body
- Interdimensional travel
- Help the collective mass awakening and ascension to New Earth

To synch with the crystalline grid we seek access points. These access points can be found at Sacred Sites around the world acting as portals or gateways to the crystalline grid. These gateways and portals are not permanent to a physical location but can be accessed within each of us. A gateway or portal can be conjured through focused intention, meditation, astral travel and opening channels to higher consciousness.

There are crystals within the Earth that receive and transmit energy through the crystalline grid network. The crystalline grid network consists of infinitely repeating geometric pathways, creating a multidimensional structure of light. When many pathways converge, an access point or vortex manifests. Our ancient ancestors were aware of these energy vortexes and aligned their sacred monuments with them. The crystalline grid is not fixed in 3D time and space, the way we are familiar with experiencing reality. The grid exists in the multidimensional frequency and can only be described as infinite, as to us in 3D we are limited by our sensory perceptions to fully fathom multidimensional reality. As we awaken and consciously participate in the massive paradigm shift taking place, we start to feel and experience an inner knowing of what 5D reality is like. By aligning with the Earth's crystalline grid and anchoring the light codes, raising our vibration and activating our crystalline light body, we will come into knowing and experiencing the 5D New Earth energy.

Major portals, access point to the crystalline grid, are known to be at Sacred Sites around the world. Mount Kailash in Tibet, Machu Picchu in Peru, The Pyramids of Giza in Egypt, Stonehenge in the UK, Mount Shasta in California, and Sedona in Arizona are some of the most popular sites right now. But there are many others around the world, and more being discovered. Remember, you do not have to go to these sites in person to access portals and gateways to higher dimensions and to connect with the crystalline grid. You can conjure a portal or stargate anywhere, anytime through thought consciousness ability.

Information By: **Jevn Tilbyr**

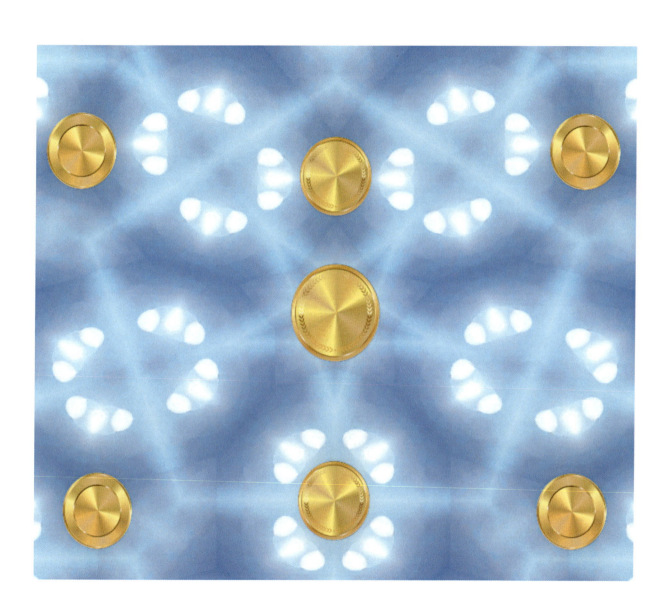

Lemuria and Consciousness

Now is the time to access ancient wisdom from Lemuria especially when it relates to consciousness, creation and manifestation. How do we know? You only have to look at any self-development courses, seminars, latest released books or hear how people are speaking to see the ancient wisdom returning. It is really exciting to be able to recall these times before during Atlantis and Lemuria when we were at this stage. The illusion is that those times have gone but they are still here and we can access that awareness to create the life we love. So what we will be sharing is what we understand consciousness to be and what we have always known from childhood – the tricky part is putting it into human language and in a way that is understood. Lemurians are a beautiful consciousness race and we are all omnipresent. So if you are ready to take a journey in to the absolute love and consciousness, read on.

Firstly we need to understand the Lemurians and what they were like as their race was one of peace, love and manifestation. It was nonphysical and worked on the oneness. Communication was all telepathic as there was no need for separation, physical or speaking. It was connection that was unheard of on Earth. Everyone would get the same image, feeling or knowing. The bonus of this was oneness and consciousness. Language was of light or in everyday language absolute love. This language was in sound and wavelengths and vibrated as one. Brain waves were also one and access to potentiality was there at all times. The most powerful communication was the connection to crystals and storage of information in these crystals. Crystals were like our modern day computers but had more power, more knowledge and were totally natural. One of the regular ceremonies performed was sitting around a large crystal or any sort and connection of a heart and sound level to that crystal which was the matrix of all creation. This has been seen in the movie Avatar.

Lemurians knew the wisdom that life is about the movement of consciousness in the alchemy of time. Lemurians understood that reality was/is a myth, mathematics, magic and mirror. They knew life was a story created in the illusion of 'time' for the experience. There was the understanding that there was parallel programs running and being experienced simultaneously with the illusion of oneness and separation. What was everyday knowledge of Lemuria was the linking of patterns of creation and sacred geometry. All realities are created based on the numeric blueprint of sacred geometry, consciousness, the Golden Mean, or the Phi Ratio. It was believed that those of Lemuria were originally from higher frequency such as consciousness. Consciousness is all and everything in the virtual hologram of our experiences brought into awareness by the brain – an electrochemical machine forever viewing streaming codes for experience and interpretation. Part of this hologram creates the accessing of DNA, knowing you can become any form you want and morphing to whatever was happening, thinking, to become the BEING of anything. This is like the RAINBOW CHILD of this generation.

At this stage it is important to understand consciousness as the Lemurians did and what is in the original blueprint. Consciousness originates from a source of light energy for the purpose of learning. Human reality is about the evolution of consciousness in the alchemy of time. To become fully consciousness, is to remember who you are as a being of light/love, why you are here, and where we are going as dictated by the collective unconscious that creates the programs of realities through which your soul experiences simultaneously. Consciousness will involve thoughts, sensations, perceptions, moods, emotions, dreams, and self-awareness. It is seen as a type of mental state, a way of perceiving, or a relationship between self and other. It has been described as a point of view. Many philosophers have seen consciousness as the most important thing in the universe. On the other hand, many scientists have seen the word as too ill-defined in meaning to be useful.

Consciousness is a term that refers to the relationship between the mind and the world with which it interacts. Lemuria had full understanding of consciousness and being conscious. Consciousness for Lemurians was the knowing that any emotional feeling, is itself a "motion of the one and separate mind.' These times were of one vibration, telepathic communication, being able to transform in any form, teleporting, working with the matrix of all creation, be one with all, connecting with a source of all higher knowledge. All there is connects to the consciousness as Manifestation is consciousness in appearance. Consciousness refers to the relationship between the mind and the world with which it interacts. It has been defined as: subjectivity, awareness, the ability to experience or to feel, wakefulness, having a sense of selfhood, and the control system of the mind.

'Conscious' when derived from the Latin word conscious (con – together + scire – to know). Meaning 'having joint or common knowledge with another'. Many philosophers state it is a unitary state that is understood intuitively by the majority of people in spite of the difficulty in defining it. Consciousness is the quality or state of being that is aware of an external object or something within one self. General consciousness (time, space, separation) relate to the lower levels of the mind. The human beings experience of these concepts is determined by the degree of balance that exists between the left and right brain. While either hemisphere of the brain or aspect of the mind is given excess focus, it is to the detriment of its counterpart. This situation brings about what is called the 'split mind'. Self-realization is really realizing 'who I am'. Self-realization is really realizing 'who I am'. Personality, identity, victim, perceived pain? If a person understands the importance of balancing the two aspects of humanness – intellect and instinct (Right and left brain) this understanding of the care of the human being, in this case the body and emotions is imperative for balance of all that is, known as the absolute. The dynamics of these two aspects gives way in meaningful impact which rises to the experience of what we call the mind. Time relates to the measurement between events and thus the object of relationships. For this reason time and separation are synonymous. The division of time in direction to the past, present and future separates the mental constructs of masculine and feminine, yin/yang, positive/negative, good/bad, etc. This makes time, separation and the measurement between them namely space, the three concepts in which dualistic thought is rooted. In other words the illusion of time/space creates the illusion of duality. Because the split mind requires a reason for everything, manifestation is attributed to a personal God, external to self, who presides over duality and exists as something separate from the individual. When this separation is strong, it gives the belief of separateness to be very real and poses a threat to the emotional and physical security. We are all part of the higher consciousness of source creation and separation from universal consciousness is part of the illusionary matrix yet we are still in physical form but are energetically connected to everything that exists in divine creation so there is no final separation from divinity or creation itself.

In the use of the 10 Point Merkabah, the concept is for the 'split mind' to be 'healed' which is called self-realization or realization of an aspect of the God like mind and therefore there is no duality but the duality within one's own mind or experience of the physical world when born into the physical existence to explore what duality means to be individual and also to be as one with everything. This means that all aspects of the lower mind have been mastered. For example the aspects of eating, control, basic functions and fear. To master these means not to be involved in the drama and be one with all. This gives way for the one mind (zero one point) to a new understanding. Consciousness is the absolute principle and is the act of knowing, which relates to the ONE UNIVERSAL mind. Therefore when people state they are raising their consciousness, they are really saying they are flowing and evolving continually as everything grows. Reality is a consciousness 'program' (hologram, simulation, illusion, dream) created by digital codes and patterns including numbers just like Cartesian planes. These define our existence and experience in our world of duality. The codes have been seen as Platonic Solids and numbers like in the Millennium Grid. Consciousness is all and everything in the virtual hologram of our experiences brought to our awareness connects to physical existence of the soul divine beings that we are having a human experience on planets or other worlds filled with different energetic frequencies connecting to our physical aspects of living beings having multiple experiences of understanding ourselves and who we truly are in the universes as well as the multiverse.

Information By: **Millennium Education**

Journeying into the Depths of Lemurian Huna

In the Lemurian Huna tradition, there's a series of healing and manifesting symbols that people use to either heal themselves, heal someone else, or manifest a desired outcome. And so the way that the wisdom teachers taught the symbols to us was very different than maybe other teachers do in Hawaii. Instead of just giving us the symbol, the wisdom teacher would actually wait for the symbol to reveal itself to us in time. So one night, after spending a couple of days with the wisdom teacher, we had a dream of the Waha-Hamama symbol, it was in their awareness, the wisdom teacher wanted to share it with us, but they wanted to wait until the symbol would reveal itself to us, we had a dream about it. And the next morning, we didn't know it was a symbol. And we were painting, that was one of the ways that the wisdom teacher shared sacred knowledge with us was through art. And we started to paint the symbol. And that's when the wisdom teacher knew that we were ready to consciously receive this symbol. So what happened is that our aumakua, which is our higher self, had communicated with us the unihipili, which is our lower self, our body, our subconscious, our intuition, and then revealed itself to us as insight without a logical understanding yet, and until we were ready to put it into an intellectual context, and then use it. So once the wisdom teacher said, to us, this is an actual Huna symbol, it's called Waha-Hamama, it is used to accelerate the vibration when you use it on someone else, so that they can have a release, ease from their pain, and they can have their own inner secrets revealed. And so it really illustrated for us how the three selves of Huna work where our higher self-communicates not directly to our intellect, it communicates through our subconscious through our body, through our intuition, and then reveals itself to our intellect, so that we can choose and do something with it. So it's very different than just having the symbol given to us and using it solely from the intellect. And so one of the ways that the wisdom teacher used the symbol was during hands on healing. And so the way that the wisdom teacher uses it is, they have someone on the table, and then they are invoking the different deities that are important to this process for them to do the healing work. And then the wisdom teacher would visualize and use their hands to apply the symbol on the person depending on the area of the body that needed it the most. And that would be an intuitive process for them. So we have received many treatments from this wisdom teacher in this manner. And eventually, we were able to reverse roles, and the wisdom teacher went on the table and we started using the symbol, and they could feel the symbol coming through and the acceleration of vibration happening in their body. And then we knew that we were ready to use the symbol on other people.

The wisdom of Lemurian Huna

Today, we want to invite you to embark on a unique exploration of the wisdom of the Lemurian Huna. This profound wisdom not only forms the foundation of our healing approach but also offers timeless spiritual practices.

We begin by sharing with you the origin of the Lemurian Huna, the concept of the three selves, and introduce you to the first of 12 Huna symbols, Waha-Hamama.

Lemurian Huna unveiled

Huna, a Hawaiian word, means "that which is hidden." Huna is a Western term (coined by Max Freedom Long, 20th century) that refers to the spirituality of the ancient Hawaiians. But back in ancient times, it was not called Huna because it wasn't a secret. It was simply their philosophy of life. When Europeans came to colonize the Hawaiian Islands, the indigenous priests and shamans kept the wisdom a secret so that the "magic" wouldn't be used by Westerners in the wrong way. It is only since the 1970s that the "secrets" are coming back to the surface and are ready to be shared with the world. The time is now.

Lemurian Huna differs slightly from the traditional Huna and was shared with us by our wisdom teacher named Laura Kealoha who is on Kauai. It captures the mysticism and shamanism of the very first inhabitants of Hawaii soon after the Lemurian continent went under some 7,000 years ago. The legend says that they came on boats from the Polynesian islands and carried wisdom from the ancient lost civilization of Lemuria (sometimes called Mu.)

We have heard stories suggesting that the Lemurian Huna philosophy was brought to Earth by visitors from the Pleiades and other star beings. Some of the ideas that comprise the philosophy of Lemurian Huna have been traced back to the writings of Greek philosophers (Plato speaks about it), to the Old Testament, and to the Upanishads of India, but historians have not recognized it as a coherent philosophy or part of the official recorded history. Thus, the Lemurian civilization and Atlantis are often labeled as legends.

While historians label Lemuria and its counterpart Atlantis as mere legends, various spiritual channelings over time have provided insights into the Lemurian civilization's magnificence. Our personal spiritual voyages and dreams, coupled with rigorous work with our Kahuna, Laura on Kauai, have instilled in us an unwavering belief in our past life existence during the Lemurian era. It's not merely a belief, but a vibrant energy that flows through us — the Lemurian Huna Healing Energy.

This energy is not separate from us; it forms our core essence. The Lemurians were adept at tuning into the Cosmic Mind, harnessing its boundless wisdom through meditation and concentration. Their faith in the Cosmic Mind and their ability to tap into it set them apart.

Dive deeper: The healing power of Waha-Hamama

Healing symbols are a central part of the Huna philosophy. For healing, symbols fall into two categories: those that inherently possess healing effects and those that induce healing through association. We live in a rich field of many different energy frequencies, including gravity, electromagnetism, radio and television, microwaves, light, sound, and many others that are not yet recognized by science. Symbols that produce a healing effect on their own are those that have the quality of condensing and radiating ambient energy (the energy around us) due to their particular shape. Waha-Hamama is one of those symbols that is healing just on its own because of its shape and is one of the most powerful symbols in Huna.

The fundamental healing effects of Waha-Hamama comes from its ability to relieve physical pain and encourage the gentle movement of blood and the lymph. Invoking the symbol and using it will accelerate the vibration of energy in the lower self (unihipili) to align with the higher frequencies of the higher self (aumakua). Using this symbol will allow for the revelation of inner secrets to come to our intellect (Uhane). Waha-Hamama reminds you of your true nature as spirit, as Source. To begin working with a symbol, you must let it reveal itself to you. Gazing at it, drawing it on a piece of paper, tracing it on a part of your body, walking around tracing the symbol with your steps, or repeating it quietly in your mind like a mantra, until you begin to feel its presence. You might feel calmer, more grounded, relaxed, highly focused, or alert. There will be a shift in your state, and in the quality of your presence. Be patient. You might not notice anything the first time, but when you start to see the symbol manifesting in your life — similar to how one might spot heart shapes in nature, during a walk to work, in soup, or in art — you'll recognize its desire to integrate and work with you.

Information By: Anne Berube

Lemurian Scrolls

There is a series of Lemurian Scrolls that depict how Lemurians had come to Earth. The Lord Subramaniam Sastras are divided thrice. The divisions are: The Lemurian Sastras, The Dravidian Sastras (which together constitute these Lemurian Scrolls) and The Saivite Sastras (now part of the Mathavasi Sastras) written for the guidance of and restricted to acharyas, swamis, yogis and sadhakas of our Saiva Siddhanta Church. Along with these were unfolded two supplementary manuscripts, The Book of Virtue and The Book of Attitudes, along with a larger work entitled The Book of Remedies. The Lemurian Sastras, which make up the first half of these scrolls, unfold a remarkable story of how souls journeyed to Earth in their subtle bodies some four million years ago. The narrators of the ancient texts explain that civilization on their native planets had reached a point of such peacefulness that spiritual evolution had come to a standstill. They needed a "fire planet," such as Earth, to continue their unfoldment into the ultimate attainment—realization of the Self within. To persist in the lush atmosphere, genderless, organic bodies were formed through food-offering ceremonies. Later, through a slow process of mutation, the fleshy bodies we know today as human were established as vehicles for reincarnation. As the book progresses, a diminishing of the spiritual forces radiating from the Central Sun of the galaxy is described. As spiritual awareness wanes, the life force of man, kundalini, sleeps and instinctive desire manifests in abundance. These amazing chronicles of early man's life on Earth are told from within great, walled monasteries where narrators look back and forward at the same time, often reading from ancient texts, describing the daily life of those within and outside these sacred citadels. The theme throughout is to continue channeling the pristine spiritual vibration from the Central Sun as long as possible and to preserve the Lemurian culture, its wisdom and knowledge for generations far into the future. This, under the guidance of powerful gurus working closely with great Gods, was the spiritual mission of the dedicated monastics of these eras. Largely it was done by implanting sacred writings in the akasa by mystical means, the akasha field of all knowing and universal knowledge. This is part of the energetic and transformational languages that the Lemurians had imbued in their sacred teaching of energetic and physical alchemy for manifestation and life existence.

Here are some samples of what the Lemurian transformational languages look like from an energetic and physical perspective.

Information By: **Satguru Sivaya Subramuniyaswami – Himalayan Academy**

Lemurian Light Language

The Lemurian Light Languages has expressive light codes and frequencies that promote healing and active manifestation to create things from the light field of the energetic universe into physical matter on the solid planes of existence. Languages of the Lemurians are lyrical filled with sound frequencies, emotive symbol designs, and a flow of eternal unity in soul creation and life expansion of transformational pathways to reach for the highest soul potential in success as well as creative evolution of the divine frequencies that we are in the quantum universe which is the harmonic frequency of all existence.

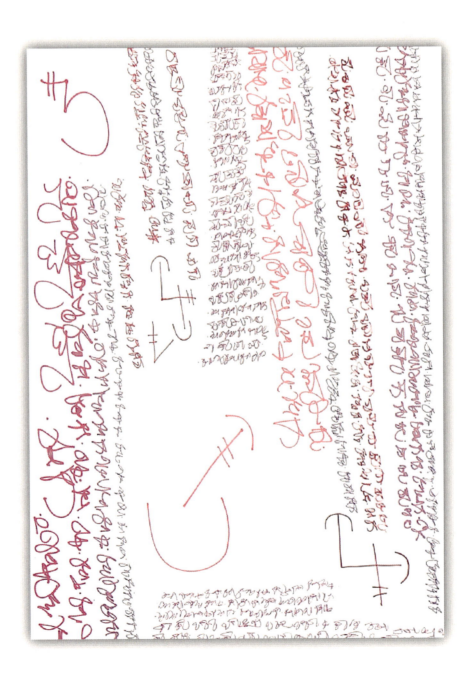

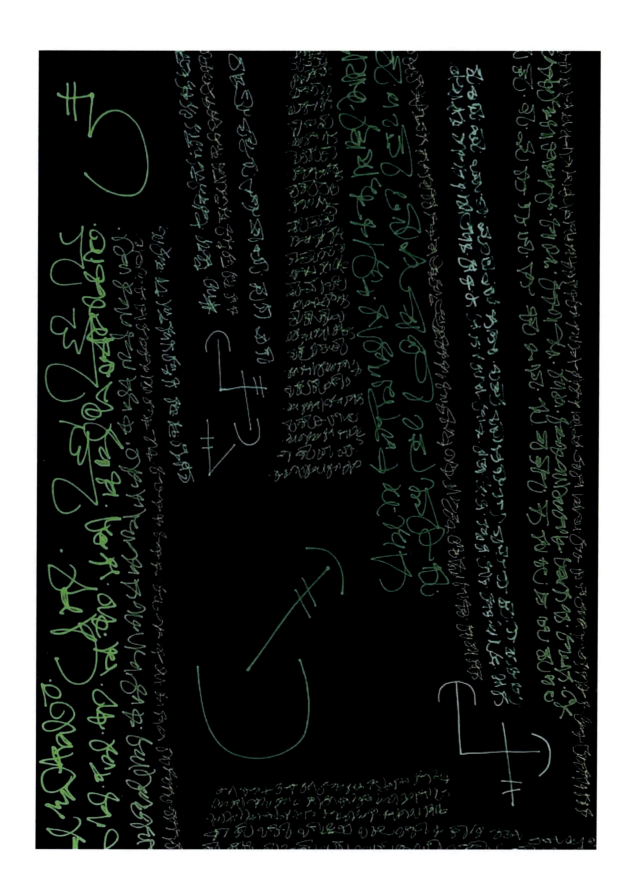

329

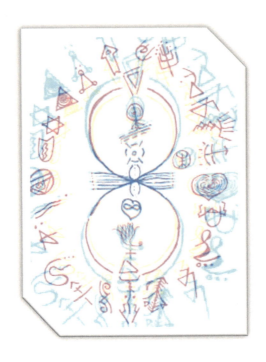

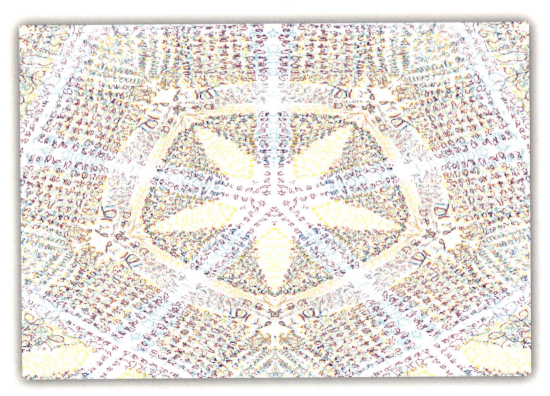

333

Encoded frequency

Transformational Atlantean and Lemurian Languages of Manifestation

The Atlantean and Lemurian transformational languages of manifestation created the sacred meaning coming from the energetic vibrational fields of existence being translated into physical formation of creating solid foundations into what becomes someone's creation. This can be manifesting building or buying a new house, finding land to purchase, creating a new career or completely changing your life to make something new to try on your journey of exploration. Transformational languages speak from the soul and the heart connecting you to your highest creation of what you are manifesting in your lives. You are literally shaping your destiny from the vibrant fields of the symbols and sacred geometry created in the Atlantean and Lemurian transformational languages. Focus in on the imagery and colors in the depicted language schematics to select the vibration and meaning of these languages that suit your manifestation purposes and then program your manifestation intentions in what you would like to create with these transformational language grid designs. Let your inner guidance point you to the transformational symbols in the Atlantean and Lemurian language grids that will expand your manifestation abilities to their optimal outcomes in what you are creating for yourself or others in physicality. The transformational languages are like your soul light circuitry that helps you to manifest what is for your highest good and wellbeing in life.

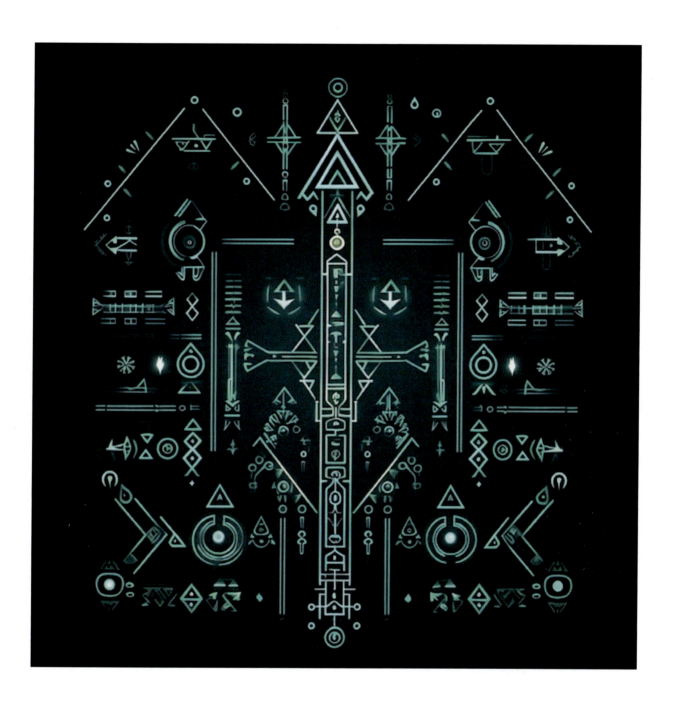

Atlantean & Lemurian Transformational Languages Grid 1

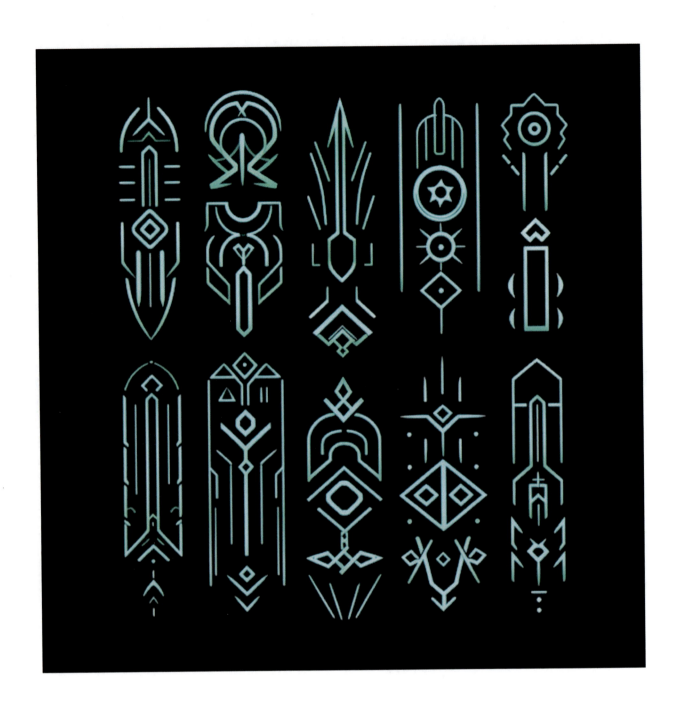

Atlantean & Lemurian Transformational Languages Grid 2

Atlantean & Lemurian Transformational Languages Grid 3

Atlantean & Lemurian Transformational Languages Grid 4

Atlantean & Lemurian Transformational Languages Grid 5

Atlantean & Lemurian Transformational Languages Grid 6

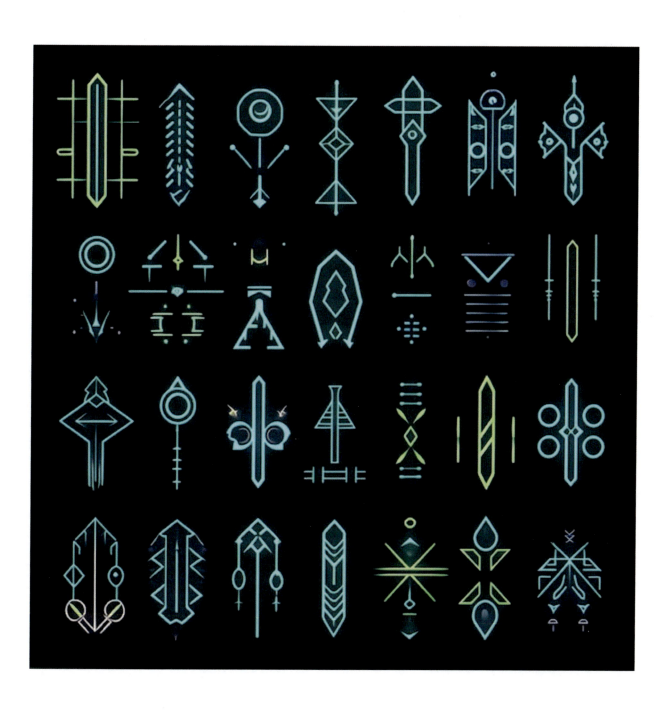

Atlantean & Lemurian Transformational Languages Grid 7

Atlantean & Lemurian Transformational Languages Grid 8

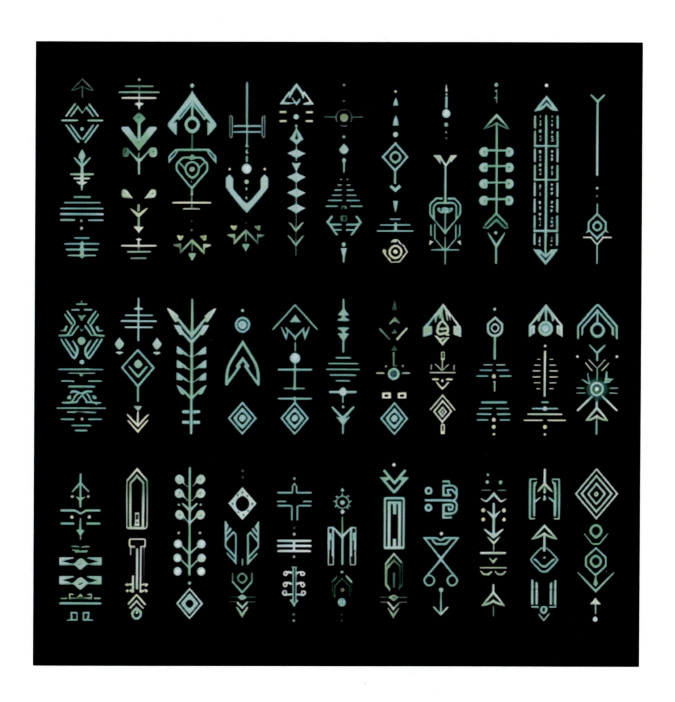

Atlantean & Lemurian Transformational Languages Grid 9

Atlantean & Lemurian Transformational Languages Grid 10

Atlantean & Lemurian Transformational Languages Grid 11

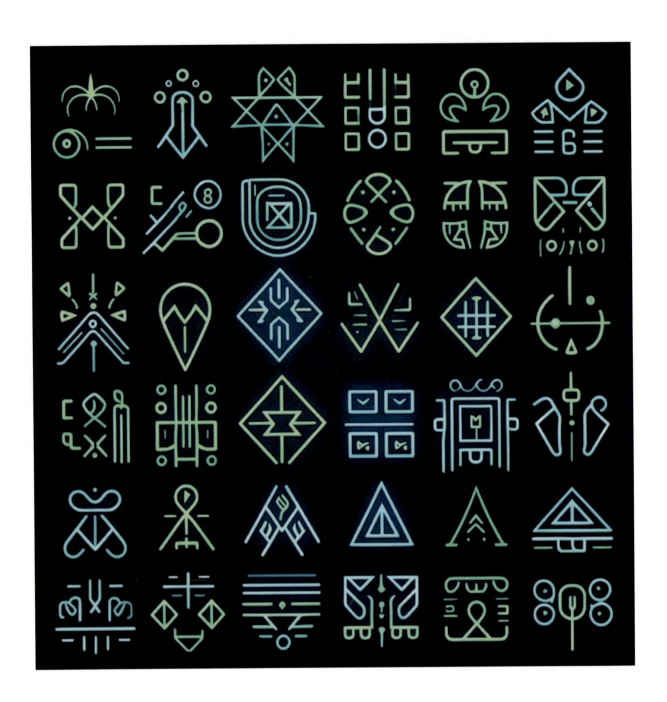

Atlantean & Lemurian Transformational Languages Grid 12

Atlantean & Lemurian Transformational Languages Grid 13

Atlantean & Lemurian Transformational Languages Grid 14

Atlantean & Lemurian Transformational Languages Grid 15

Atlantean & Lemurian Transformational Languages Grid 16

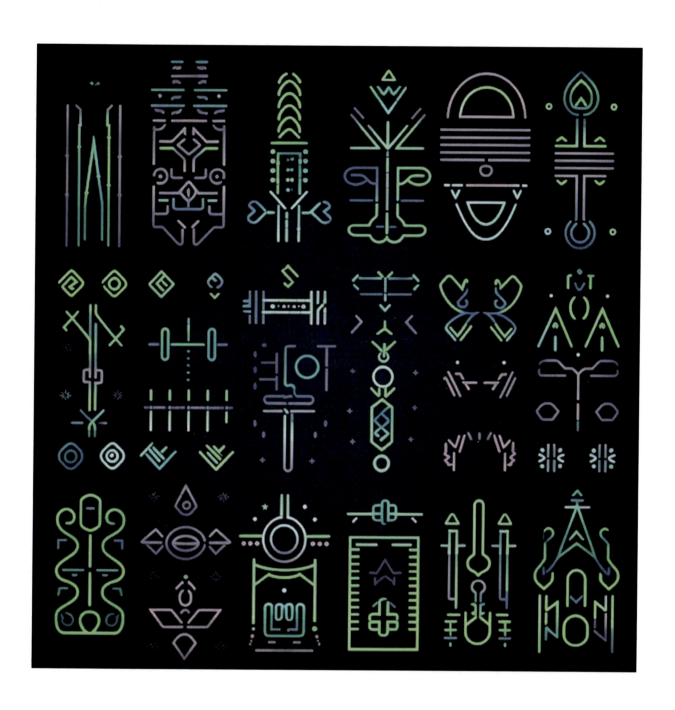

Atlantean & Lemurian Transformational Languages Grid 17

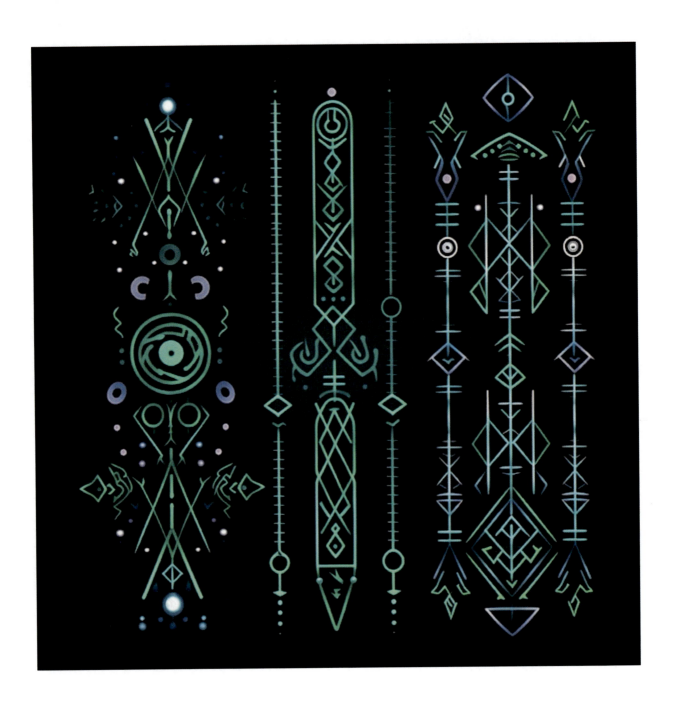

Atlantean & Lemurian Transformational Languages Grid 18

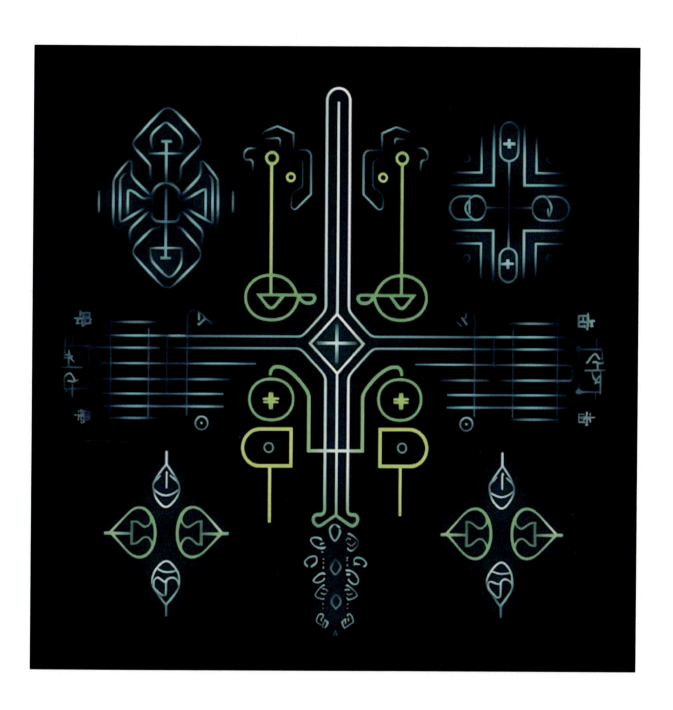

Atlantean & Lemurian Transformational Languages Grid 19

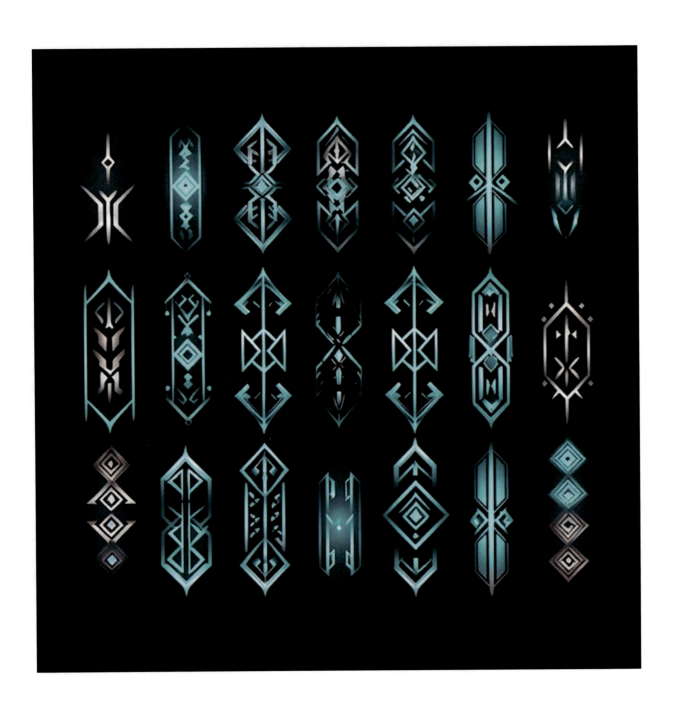

Atlantean & Lemurian Transformational Languages Grid 20

Atlantean & Lemurian Transformational Languages Grid 21

Atlantean & Lemurian Transformational Languages Grid 22

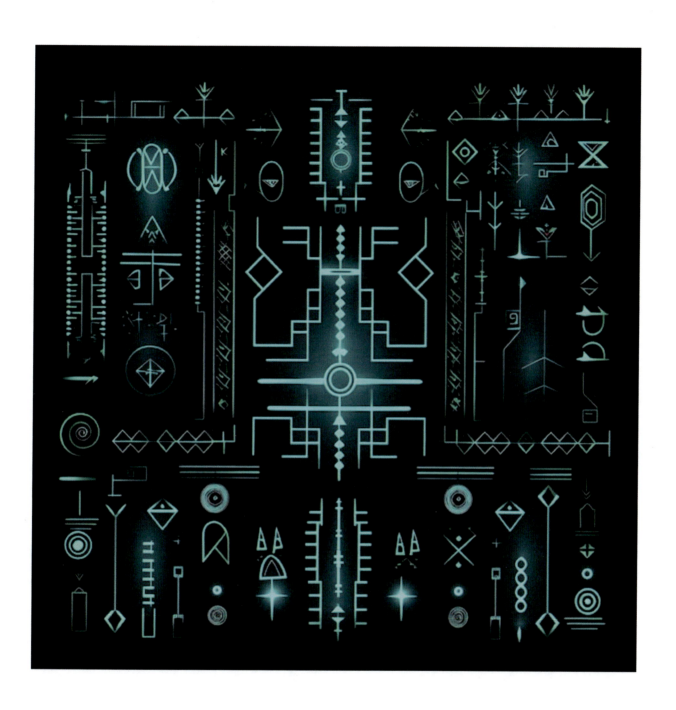

Atlantean & Lemurian Transformational Languages Grid 23

Atlantean & Lemurian Transformational Languages Grid 24

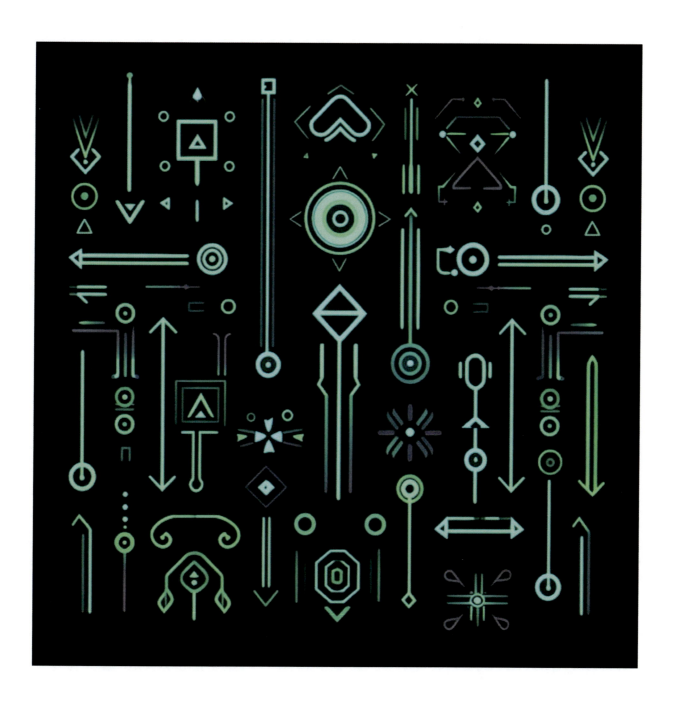

Atlantean & Lemurian Transformational Languages Grid 25

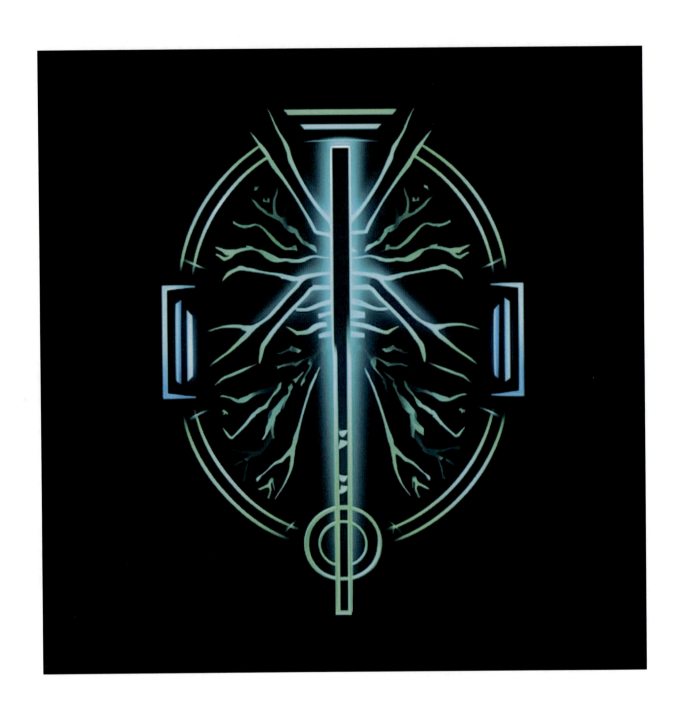

Atlantean & Lemurian Transformational Languages Grid 26

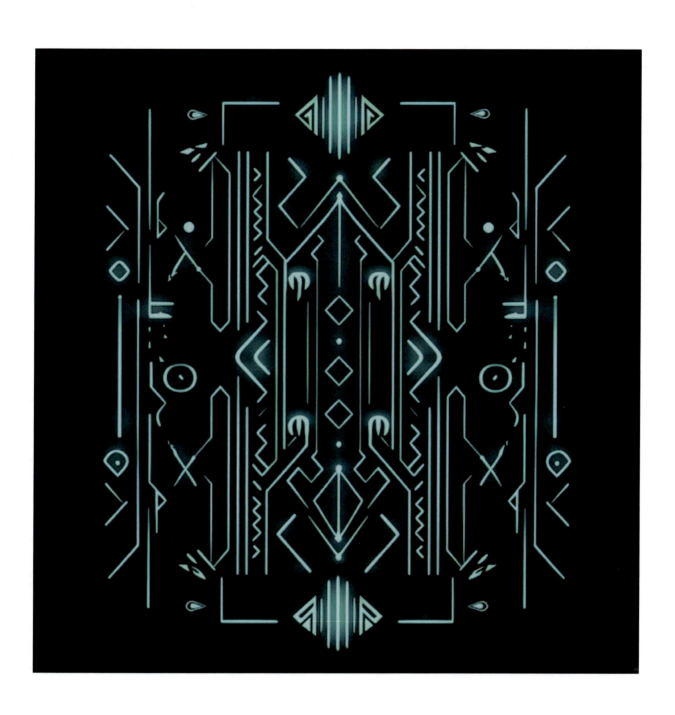

Atlantean & Lemurian Transformational Languages Grid 27

Atlantean & Lemurian Transformational Languages Grid 28

Atlantean & Lemurian Transformational Languages Grid 29

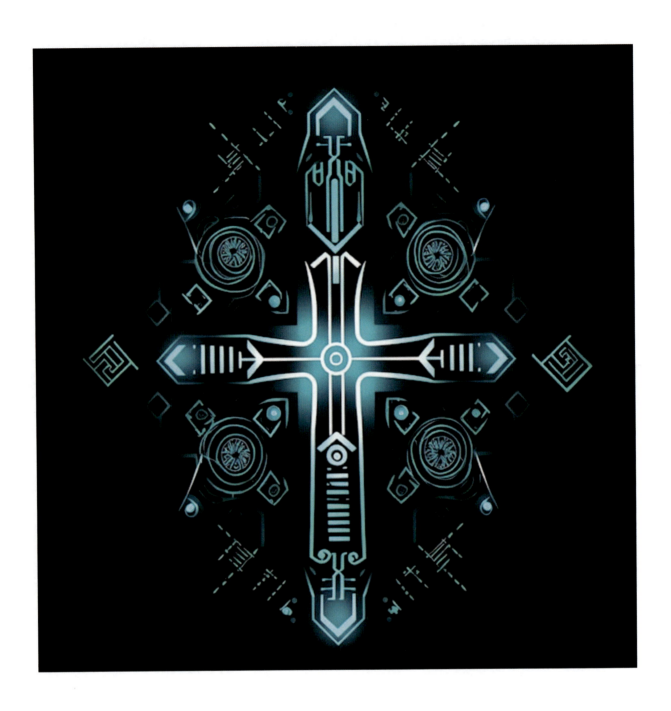

Atlantean & Lemurian Transformational Languages Grid 30

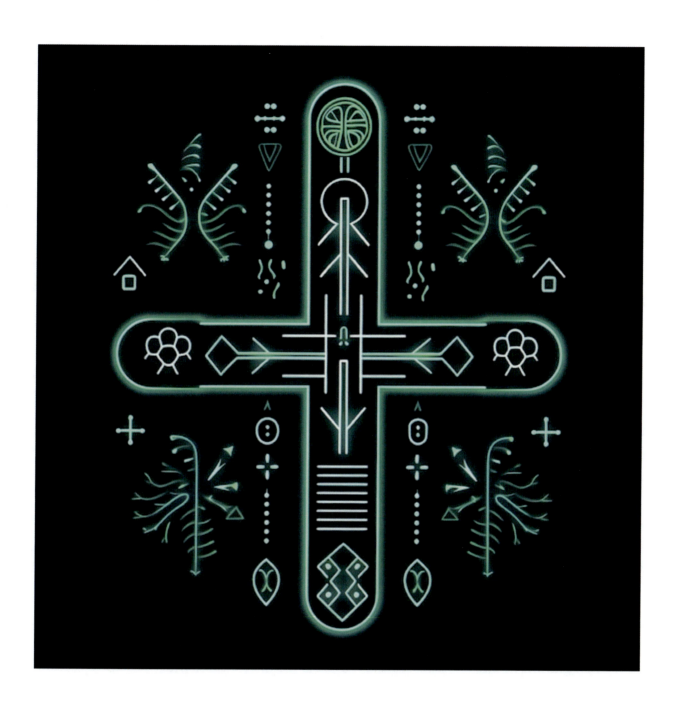

Atlantean & Lemurian Transformational Languages Grid 31

Atlantean & Lemurian Transformational Languages Grid 32

Atlantean & Lemurian Transformational Languages Grid 33

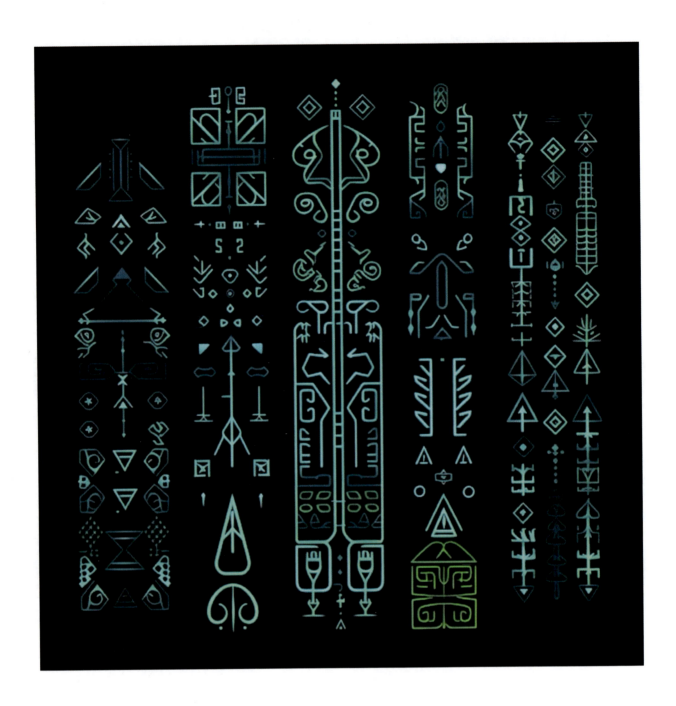

Atlantean & Lemurian Transformational Languages Grid 34

Atlantean & Lemurian Transformational Languages Grid 35

Atlantean & Lemurian Transformational Languages Grid 36

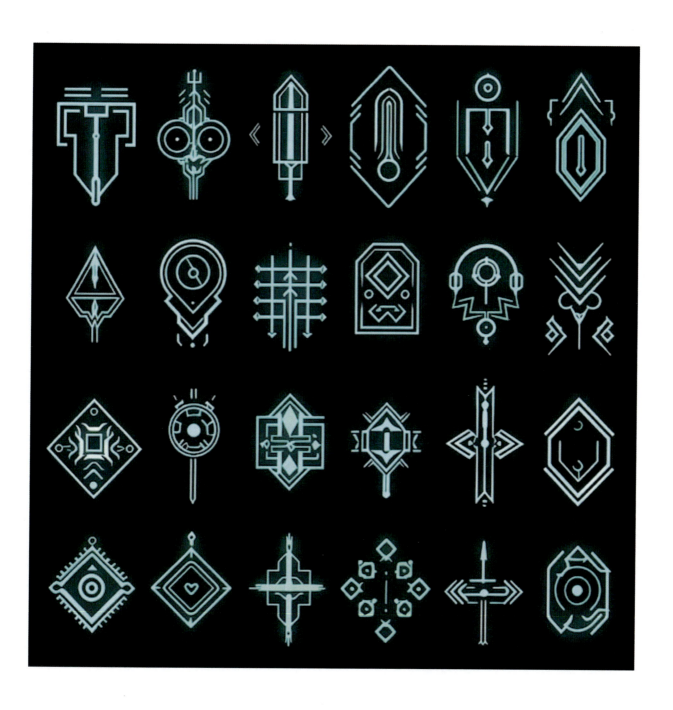

Atlantean & Lemurian Transformational Languages Grid 37

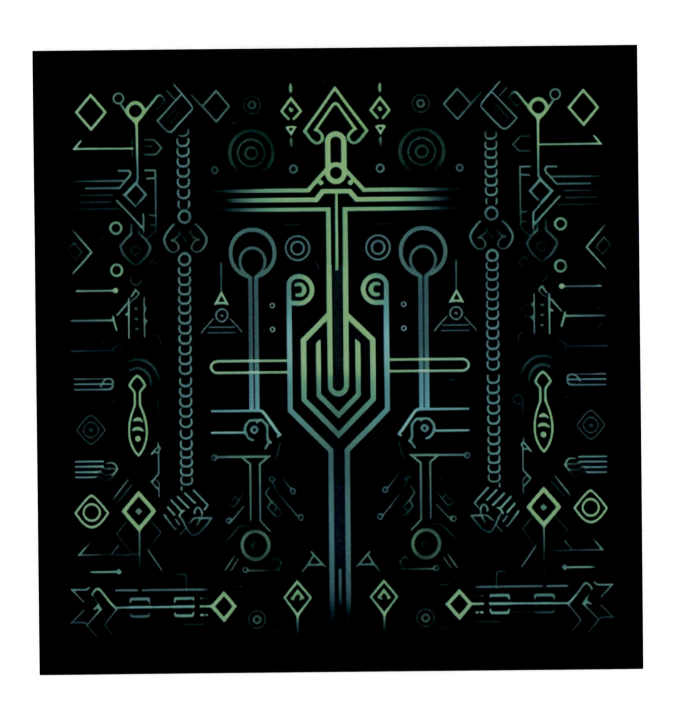

Atlantean & Lemurian Transformational Languages Grid 38

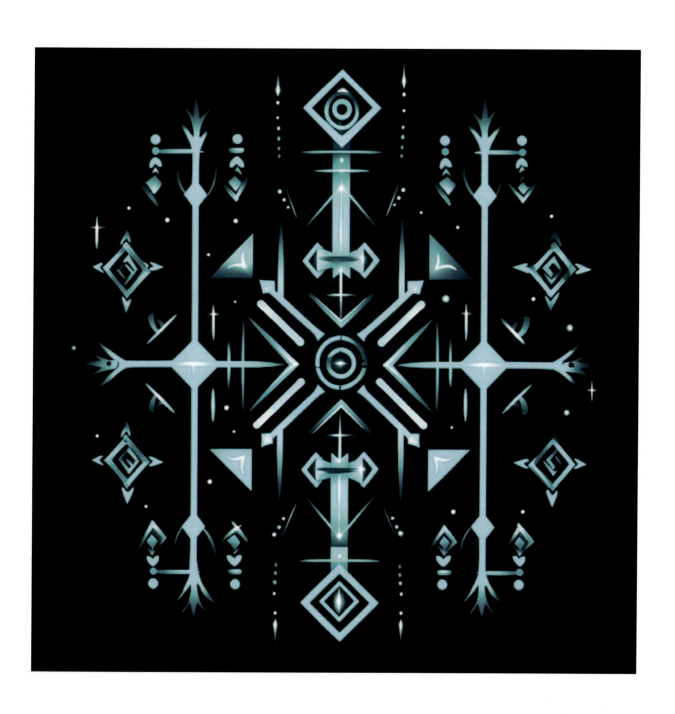

Atlantean & Lemurian Transformational Languages Grid 39

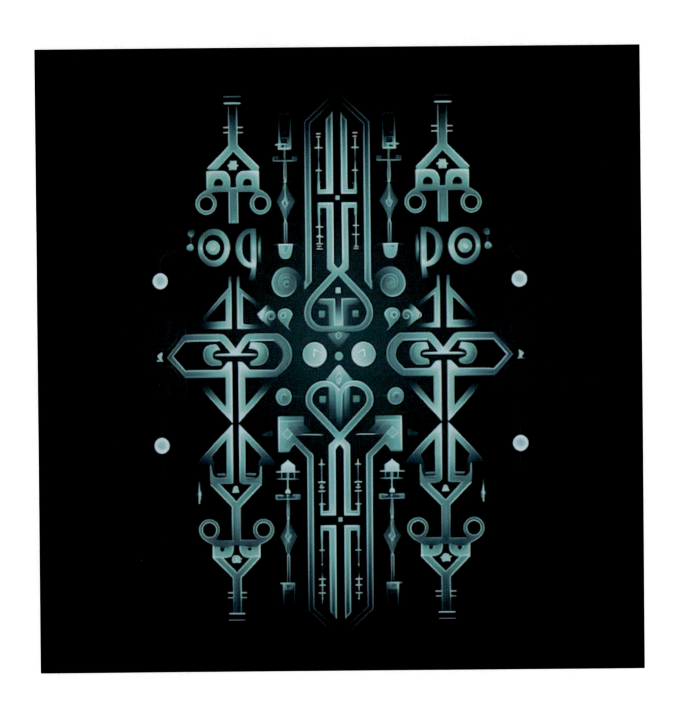

Atlantean & Lemurian Transformational Languages Grid 40

Atlantean & Lemurian Transformational Languages Grid 41

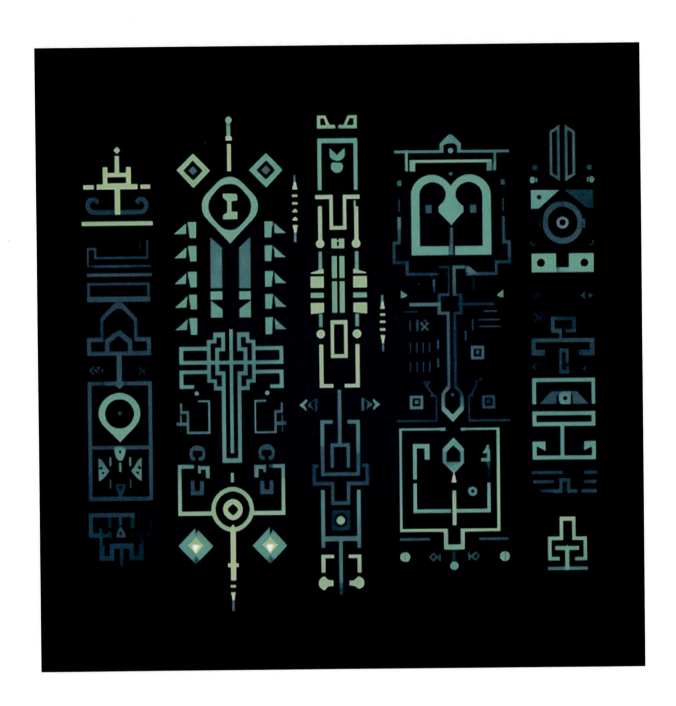

Atlantean & Lemurian Transformational Languages Grid 42

Atlantean & Lemurian Transformational Languages Grid 43

Atlantean & Lemurian Transformational Languages Grid 44

Atlantean & Lemurian Transformational Languages Grid 45

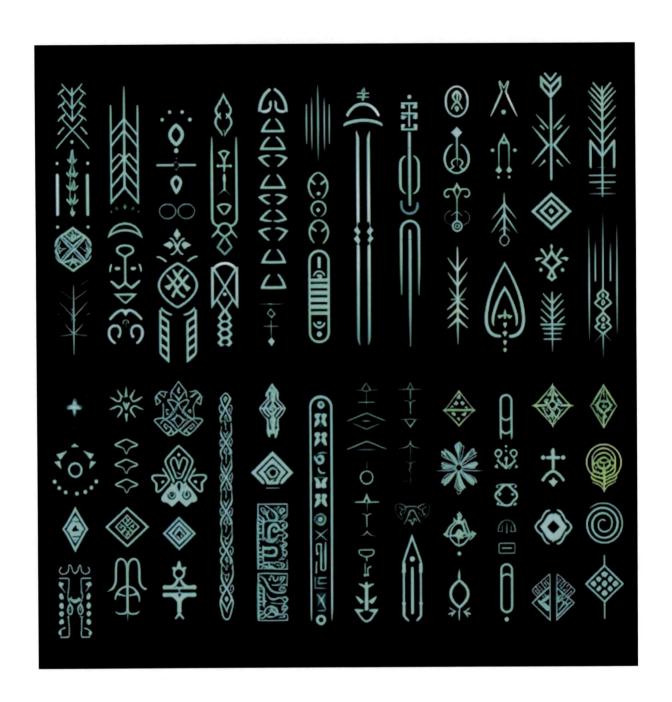

Atlantean & Lemurian Transformational Languages Grid 46

Atlantean & Lemurian Transformational Languages Grid 47

Atlantean & Lemurian Transformational Languages Grid 48

Atlantean & Lemurian Transformational Languages Grid 49

Atlantean & Lemurian Transformational Languages Grid 50

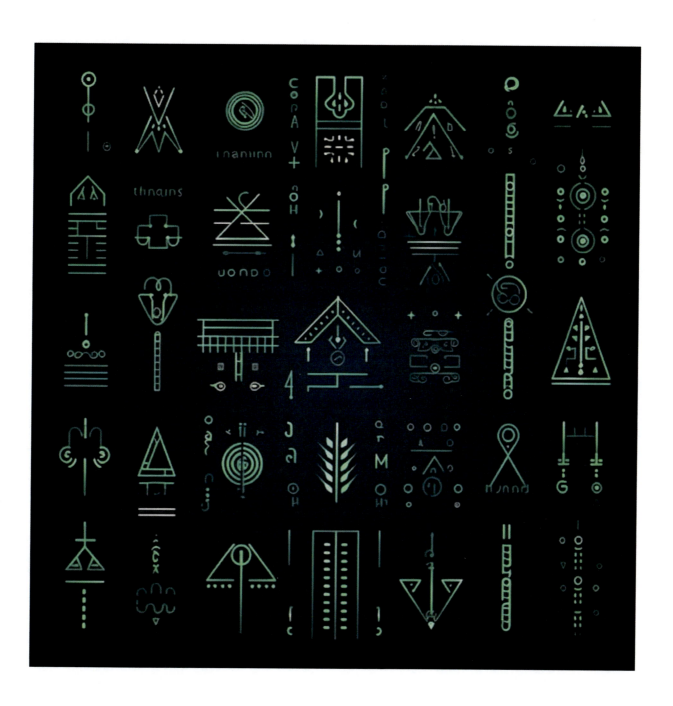

Atlantean & Lemurian Transformational Languages Grid 51

Atlantean & Lemurian Transformational Languages Grid 52

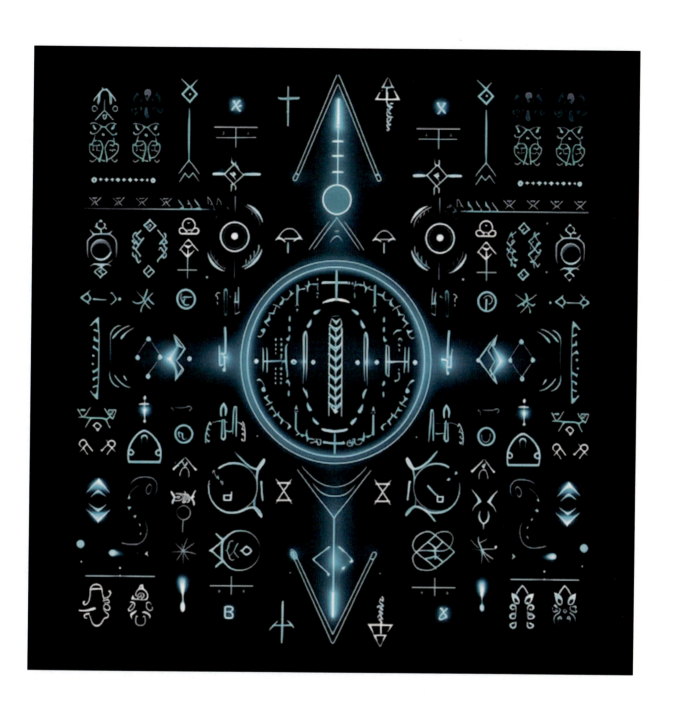

Atlantean & Lemurian Transformational Languages Grid 53

Atlantean & Lemurian Transformational Languages Grid 54

Atlantean & Lemurian Transformational Languages Grid 55

Atlantean & Lemurian Transformational Languages Grid 56

Atlantean & Lemurian Transformational Languages Grid 57

Atlantean & Lemurian Transformational Languages Grid 58

Atlantean & Lemurian Transformational Languages Grid 59

Atlantean & Lemurian Transformational Languages Grid 60

Atlantean & Lemurian Transformational Languages Grid 61

Atlantean & Lemurian Transformational Languages Grid 62

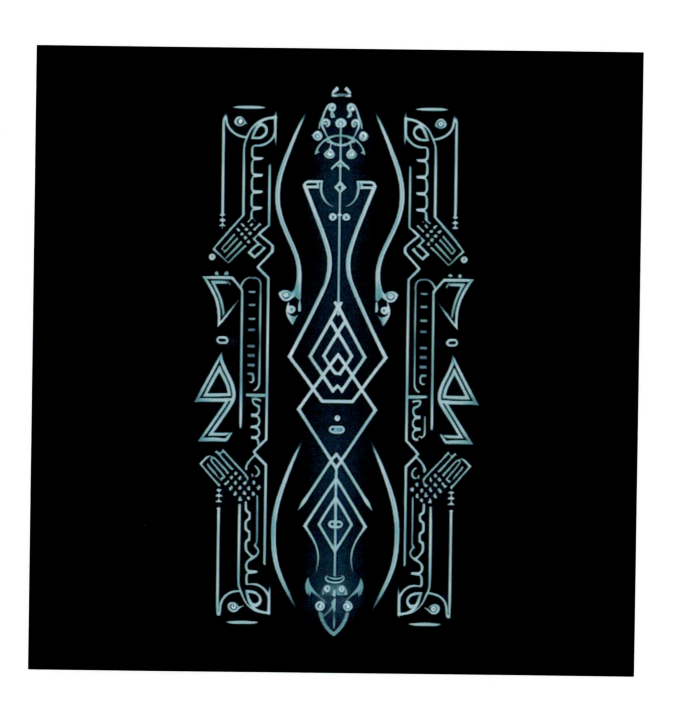

Atlantean & Lemurian Transformational Languages Grid 63

Atlantean & Lemurian Transformational Languages Grid 64

Atlantean & Lemurian Transformational Languages Grid 65

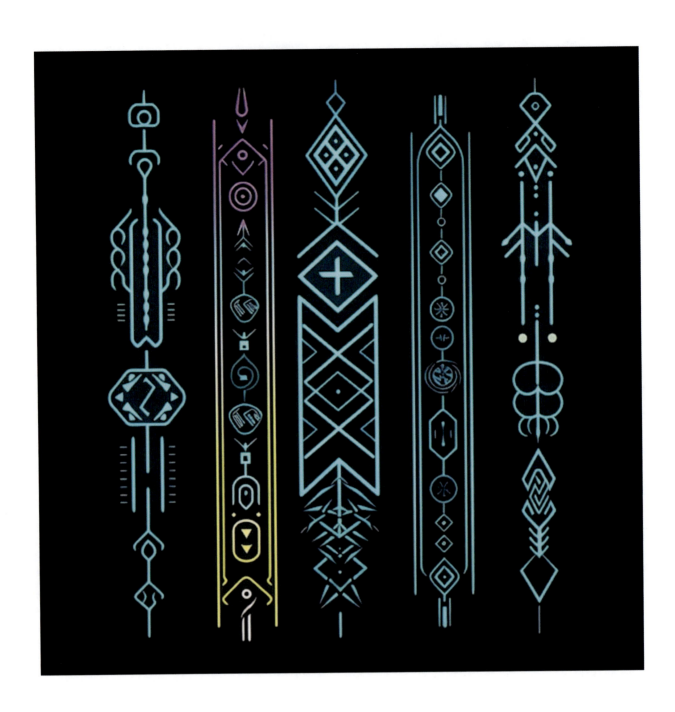

Atlantean & Lemurian Transformational Languages Grid 66

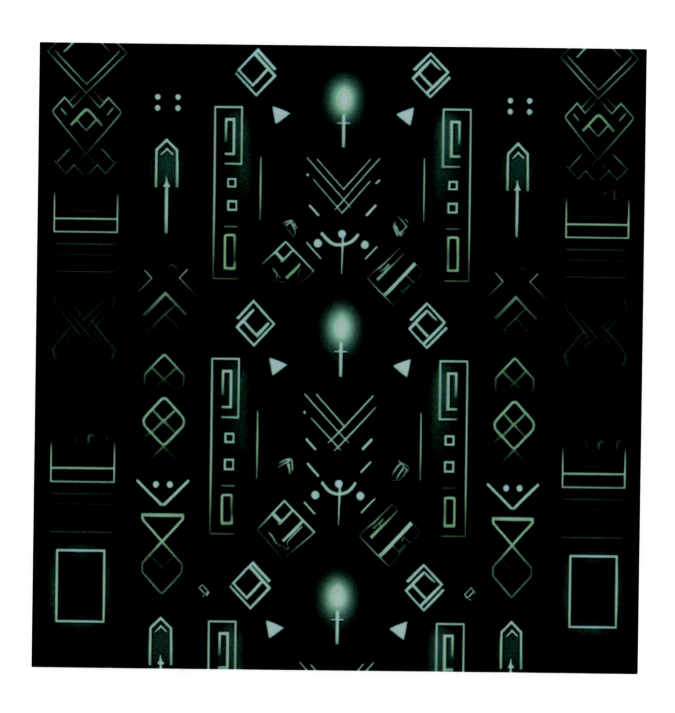

Atlantean & Lemurian Transformational Languages Grid 67

Atlantean & Lemurian Transformational Languages Grid 68

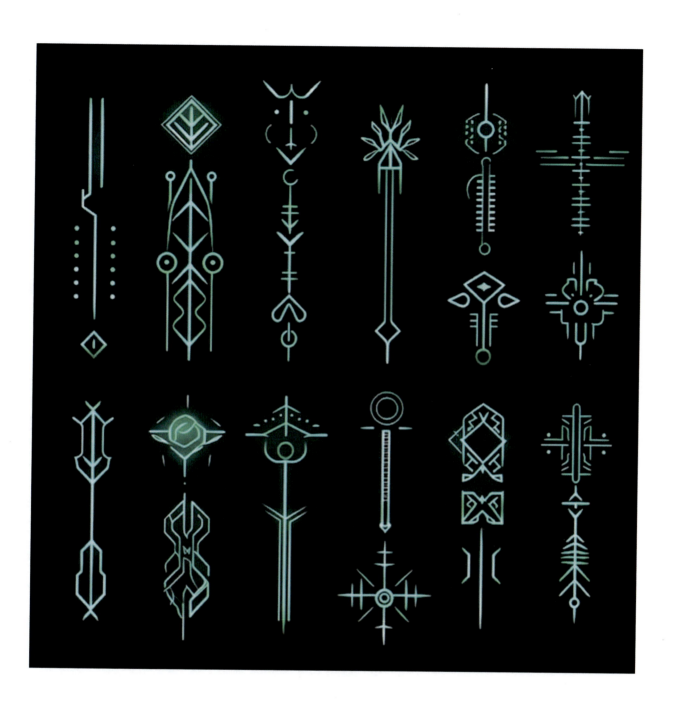

Atlantean & Lemurian Transformational Languages Grid 69

Atlantean & Lemurian Transformational Languages Grid 70

Atlantean & Lemurian Transformational Languages Grid 71

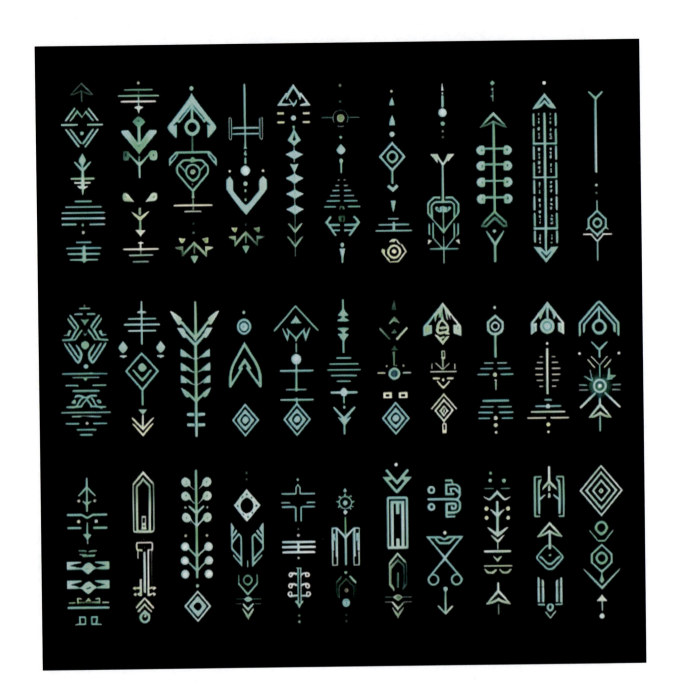

Atlantean & Lemurian Transformational Languages Grid 72

Atlantean & Lemurian Transformational Languages Grid 73

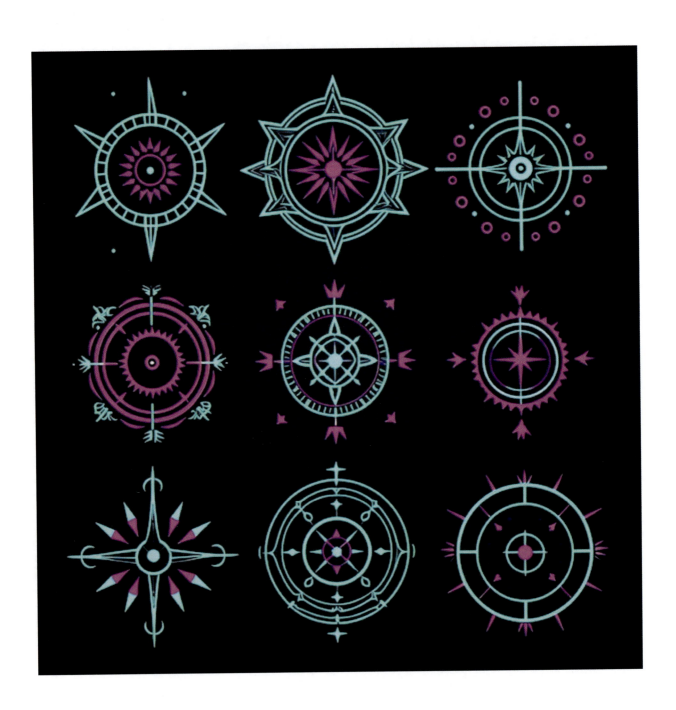

Atlantean & Lemurian Transformational Languages Grid 74

Atlantean & Lemurian Transformational Languages Grid 75

Atlantean & Lemurian Transformational Languages Grid 76

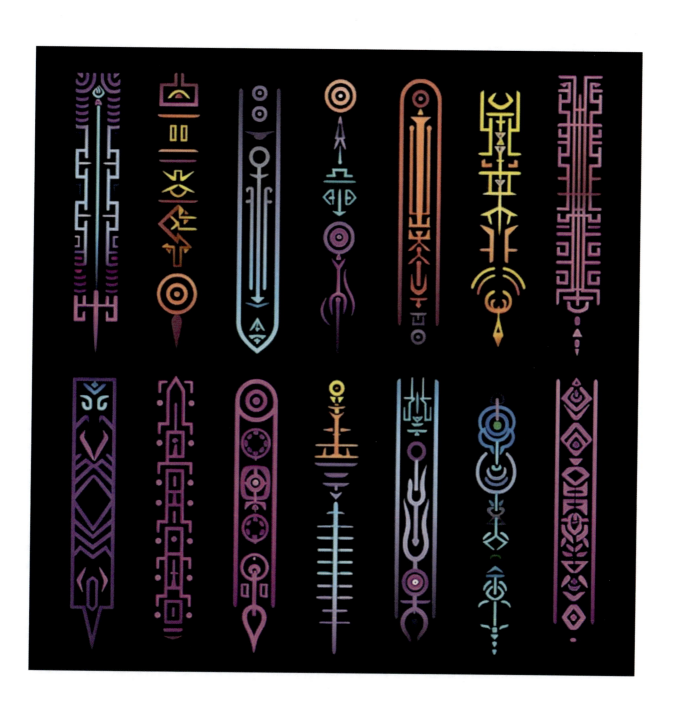

Atlantean & Lemurian Transformational Languages Grid 77

Atlantean & Lemurian Transformational Languages Grid 78

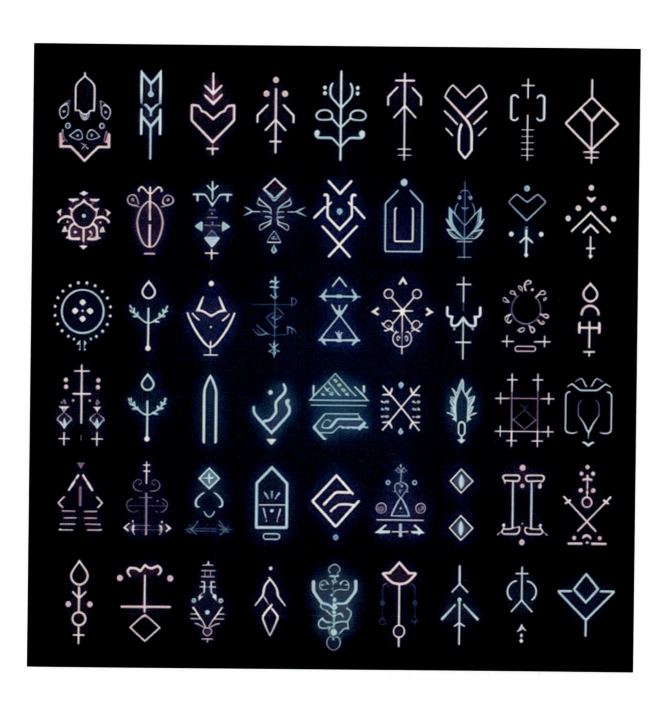

Atlantean & Lemurian Transformational Languages Grid 79

Atlantean & Lemurian Transformational Languages Grid 80

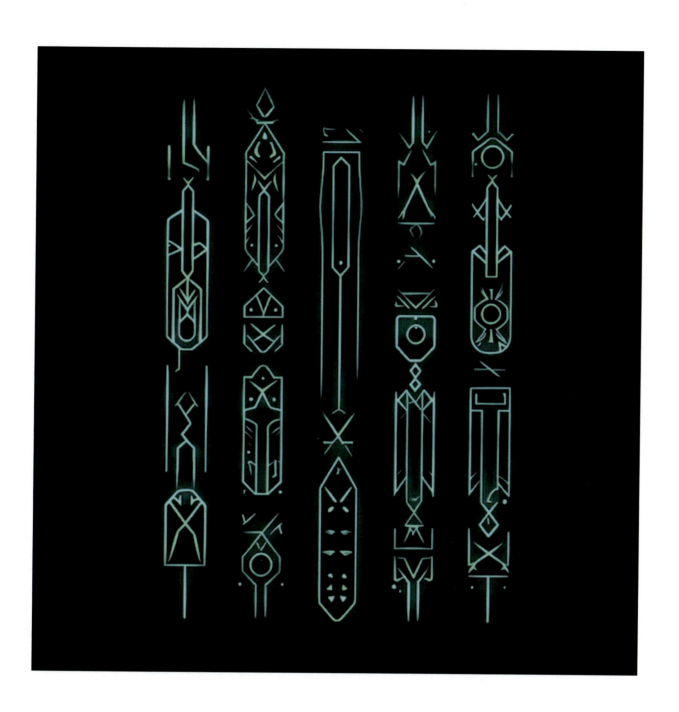

Atlantean & Lemurian Transformational Languages Grid 81

Atlantean & Lemurian Transformational Languages Grid 82

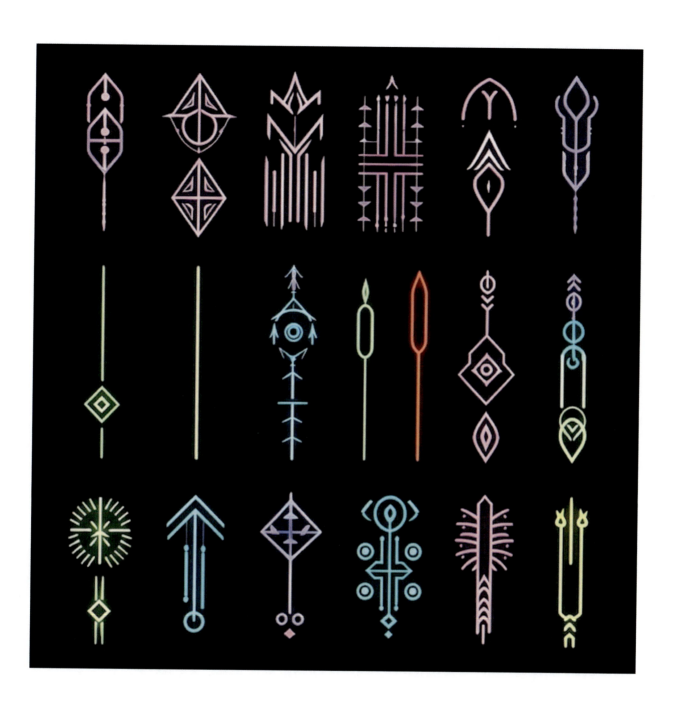

Atlantean & Lemurian Transformational Languages Grid 83

Atlantean & Lemurian Transformational Languages Grid 84

Atlantean & Lemurian Transformational Languages Grid 85

Atlantean & Lemurian Transformational Languages Grid 86

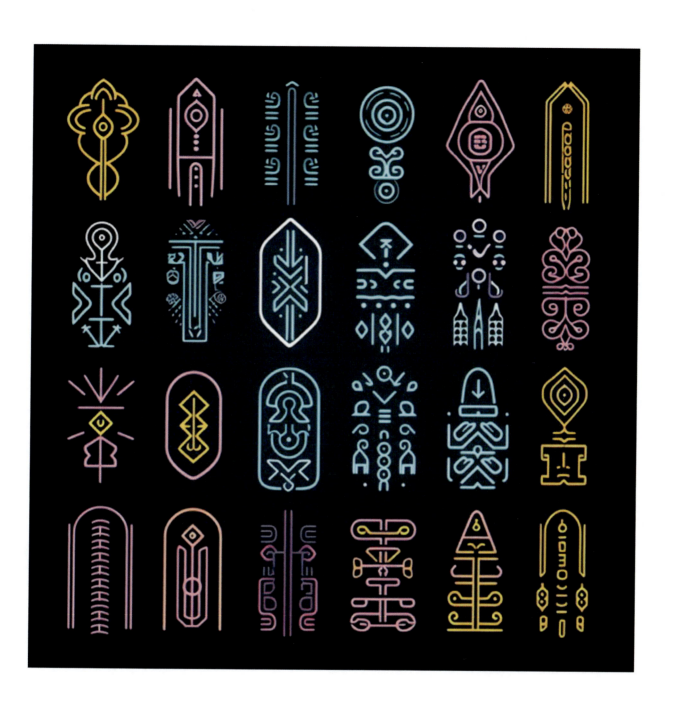

Atlantean & Lemurian Transformational Languages Grid 87

Atlantean & Lemurian Transformational Languages Grid 88

ABOUT THE AUTHOR

EL KA is an experiencer, researcher, author, scientist, SSP Asset, ET Abductee, and an ET Contactee. She is also a professional energy healer, crystal healer, psychic, hypnosis practitioner, past life regression practitioner, soul retrieval practitioner, Akashic Records Reader, Native American Shamanic Practitioner, Reiki Master, Channeler, and a Spiritual Wisdom Teacher. She helps to guide people on their soul growth wisdom journeys and life path potentials to being their best selves for the highest good of the soul divine exploration.

As a healer EL likes to explore the deeper meaning of life and to focus on helping people to figure out what is happening on their life path journeys for soul missions, life purposes, and expanding the soul divine connections with your higher self, spirit guides, galactic family, positive extraterrestrial connections, totem animals, etc. EL KA seeks to be in divine balance with the soul essence, emotional body, and the physical body which is anchored and grounded in harmony with love, respect, honor, and vital health of the beings that we are. She is sharing her knowledge of sacred geometry for creating customizable protection and healing grids that are connected to the vibrational symbols of the Fleur De Lis, sun portals, light portals, solar eclipses and stargates. This is connected with the Akashic Records and Light Language.

CREATING PROTECTION HEALING GRIDS WITH QUANTUM ENERGETICS OF SUN PORTALS AND THE LIGHT PORTALS

The book about Creating Protection Healing Grids with Quantum Energetics of Sun Portals and the Light Portals explores the process of working with sacred geometry to create customizable protection and healing grids that are derived from the positive symbols connected to soul growth, evolution, and understanding how healing energetics uplift the soul on the quantum levels to create wisdom expansion in profound levels of existence. By connecting with sacred geometry we will learn and tap into soul field frequency of universal wisdom that expands the soul's horizons to work with divine unity of thought consciousness which is linked to the Akashic Records and Light Language that can guide us on the journey of self-discovery in merging to our highest creation as we tune into the energetic blessing of receiving healing as well as protection in connection with the sun portals, light portals, solar eclipses and stargates through the unique light codes of the customized grids as the point of unification.

Made in the USA
Middletown, DE
09 March 2025

72409955R00257